EVERYTHING
HAS
ITS TIME

*To everything, there is a season, and a time to every purpose
under the heaven: (Eccles.3:1 KJV)*

YVONNE D. BUNDRAGE

Presented To

_____

From

_____

Date

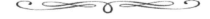

_____

ISBN: 978-1-0881-1941-9

Printed in the United States of America

Published by Bookmarketeers.com

This book is dedicated in memory of
my mother, my son, and all
who are going through
adversities, trials,
life's challenges,
and struggles.

Acknowledgments

Foremost, I want to thank God for placing it in my heart to write this book, the patience to follow through, the wisdom and guidance along the way, the right resources to complete the task, and for having your anointing and favor in my life. Thank you for everything.

To my caring, loving, and supportive husband, you were my most incredible support because I could not share my book writing with anyone. Thank you so much for all your advice. You continued to encourage me throughout. You have been a great help, and I can't thank you enough for what you have assisted and inspired me to accomplish.

A huge thank you to Joel Osteen, Pastor of Joel Osteen Radio and Ministries, for every time I would get into my car, those motivating words I needed to hear would be on the station at the time. Thank you for when I would go walking and listen to you on my phone on Sirius XM, how amazing it would be as though it was destined for me to hear those messages. Without a doubt, I could not have completed this task without hearing your inspiring and encouraging words. Those words were confirmations. You are indeed a blessing and a remarkable man of God.

Thank you to all at Book Marketeers who made this happen. Amy Miller, Book Marketing Specialist, thank you so much for convincing me to allow your publishing agency to format, edit, proofread, design, and publish my book. It has not been easy. (Basecamp) team, Eminey, Tessa, Anne, and all of you guys, thank you for your patience with me when I continued to make changes; I know I was driving you all insane. This could not have happened without you all. Your tolerance of me was well appreciated when I would not follow your instructions and make the changes in the comment section, making the formatting harder for you all.

Katherine Gilbert, in the short time you have been there, you have been splendid, and I thank you. Chris Matthew, thank you so much for my book cover, I'm so thankful to you all. Forgive me, this is my first book, and I had to figure it all out. Again, thank you all for your patience with me. You all have been a blessing. I know you all are saying, "Thank God it's completed."

My loving daughter, thank you for recommending the software Grammarly. It has been a great benefit. Thank you, and I appreciate all of the other ways you have supported and assisted me in making this book writing a success.

My second oldest brother, thank you so much for providing me with information for the questions I was asking and not wanting to know why I needed it. Thank you also for your teachings as a pastor throughout the years and all your knowledge.

Thank you my third oldest brother for sharing all of your knowledge of our family history memories without knowing what I was trying to accomplish. You were a tremendous help to me. You asked me if I was writing a book after asking many questions and I played it off.

Acknowledging my other two brothers, whom I did not ask questions about the family during my writing. It wasn't to overlook you two, it would have been too obvious, and I would not have been able to be discreet enough to hide why I was asking questions. I was not to share with anyone my book writing; therefore, it was easier to sneak questions in with the other two, because we talk more often.

My sister and friend, I apologize for the many times you would call and ask what I was doing or what I'd been up to and my response would be,

"Nothing much, the same… on the computer." I know my sister was probably thinking, I was at the Hard Rock. I may have mentioned that I was working on a project. This is my project.

Table of Contents

Preface

I've been listening to Joel Osteen Ministries for several years on Joel Osteen Radio Sirius XM in my car, on my phone, and when I walk three miles every other day. In some of his messages, when he's talking about what God will do in your life, he'd say; *you will find that husband, you will start that business, you will write that book, among other things.* In another message, he may say, *you will break that addiction, and it will happen suddenly.*

He would also say, God will take you places you never dreamed you would go; it will happen much sooner than you think because we serve a supernatural God. You do not need the experience or education for what God has anointed you to do. He's going to bring out your gifts and talents. He's going to show you His blessings. Everyone around you will know you have the favor of God in your life; now, you must get it down into your spirit and believe it. I would ask myself, whom is he talking to? What am I going to do?

My husband and I started going to the Hard Rock Casino gambling in Tampa, Florida, in 2007. It was around 3.5 years after the death of my son. It began as a casual night out and ended up as an addiction that was difficult to break, and we struggled with it. I'd self-ban myself, only to find myself back.

On the evening of April 25, 2022, we were pulling into the driveway of our home after returning from another disappointing trip at the Hard Rock; where we would continue to feed the slot machines our money, getting nothing in return, or when we would get something, we would play it back.

It came to me plain and clear to write a book. I do not consider myself a writer. Trusting God put that desire in my heart; the following day I began writing my manuscript, not having any idea what I'd write about. Beginning with one theme, I didn't get very far. Researching the least amount of words I would need to write a book, I told my husband there was no way I can recall enough memory to note that many words. He said, "Yes, you can." He advised me to take the writing in a different direction, which I needed because, following his advice, I took off with it. Being inspired every day to write, because I knew that message came from God.

While writing the book, I'd listen to Joel Osteen while walking, then, when I would get into our car, I'd hear the same messages, and it seemed like he was talking to me. Never would I've imagined, sitting down and gathering this many memories to write a book. Then I continued to get confirmation from his messages until I completed the book. This was not a dream of mine. It had to be God. He guided me, and I'd listen to Joel Osteen, on Sirius XM, on my telephone, and in my car, at the right time to hear those messages that inspired and encouraged me. I've always listened to him, but it seemed to be different during my writing. Since April 25, 2022, we have not revisited the Hard Rock.

No one could've told me on April 25, 2022, before pulling into our driveway, that I would write a book. I'm ecstatic at what God is doing right now. It is amazing. I obeyed his notion and wrote a book. I'm truly honored to honor God with my writing.

Introduction

I've heard people say God spoke to them and told them different things, and I'd never had that experience, until the evening of April 25, 2022. It was placed on my heart to write a book and I know it was God. I had never experienced anything like that before.

I then prayed for God to guide me to make certain I would write what would be pleasing to Him and there'd be testimonies to help someone else, so God will get the glory. It has indeed been healing for me.

To every thing, there is a season and a time for every purpose under the heaven: (Eccles. 3:1 KJV). This book is about life's adversities, challenges, struggles, trials, faith in their midst, and resilience because God is with us and will never leave or forsake us. Life happens to us all. Throughout our lives, we are all going to experience trials. Trials come to test our faith. With our faith being tested, it produces endurance. Endurance is the power to stand amid adversities without giving up.

My mother struggled with her marriages throughout her life and the trials she went through with my father and stepfather taught me endurance. Learning about my second oldest brother's healing and my grandmother's strong religious beliefs helped me to have stronger faith. Her sister, my grandaunt, in her later years, faced a situation too much for her to deal with. Also, it was heartbreaking to witness my grandmother's son, my uncle, struggling after returning from the military. It taught me how to continue to have faith after seeing my loved ones go through adversities.

My trials continue to come to test my faith and started when I was younger. I struggled with insecurities, and being called names, and made fun of which also taught me endurance. Giving birth at a young age, then later, his tragic death. How God used our little dog to help our daughter. Being tested throughout our marriage. Then the challenges I experienced through my many jobs. My struggle with gambling. Then, learned the truth about something I've questioned all my life.

Those life experiences have shaped me and made me the individual I am today. God has allowed me to witness as well as shown me through my family and other people who He is and how everything has its time and will work out as God has planned.

Chapter One

Growing Up

On May 8, 1957, my mother gave birth to me at Manatee Memorial Hospital in Bradenton, Florida. We lived in Palmetto, Florida. I was one of six children; four older brothers and a younger sister.

We all did not share the same fathers but the same mother. Even though we shared different fathers, we never referred to one another as half-sisters or half-brothers. We are just sisters and brothers.

When I was born, the name on my birth certificate was not my father's last name. My mother had been married to my oldest and second oldest brother's father therefore, I had her married last name. My oldest brother had my mother's maiden last name. I was always curious why I did not have my father's last name. That was because they were not married at that time. I did not realize I was different until I was in kindergarten.

Around this time, questions started being asked about why my last name wasn't the same as my dad's. It must have been when my mother enrolled me in school when I attained my father's last name. He was my father, so why not have his last name? They changed my last name only through the school system, not through the courts.

Bullying

During my kindergarten years, my family lived in a subdivision called Washington Gardens in Palmetto. I was unhappy living in that neighborhood because of this boy who bullied me daily. And because it was a long way and we had to walk to school and back, this boy would have me running home. He would chase me, trying to start a fight.

He was not the only bully who taunted me, because it was this older girl who would braid my hair; while braiding it, she would pull it and slap me across my head when she felt I did not turn my head straight. She was always picking on me.

My neighbors growing up

With my mother and dad making decent earnings in 1963, they built a home in the Harrison Subdivision in Palmetto. The house they built was a three-bedroom, two-and-a-half-bath home. It had a large family room, a pleasant-sized kitchen, a big living room, a carport, and an outside utility room. My sister and I shared a room with twin beds. My brothers shared a room with one bunk bed and one twin bed. A half bath adjoined their room. My parents had their main bedroom. Back then, most homes in black neighborhoods did not have air conditioning. It wasn't until years when my oldest brother installed air conditioning as a gift to our mother.

A few vacant lots were available in our neighborhood. The house already built next door to the right of us is where a school teacher, her husband, a chef cook, and their two sons lived. Many envied them. As a teenager, they impressed me. They were the closest to being what we considered rich. They had a big beautiful home with a large family room and a bar, with plenty of liqueurs. There was also a large pool table in the bar room. They would have cases of coke drinks delivered to their home and would buy new cars every two or three years.

Their younger son had gotten a brand-new Pontiac Trans Am. It was gold with the black phoenix emblem on the hood. It was a sharp-looking car. His older brother drove a nice car as well. They had everything. Years later, adversities took their toll on their family. They raised their kids, giving them everything, and it ruined them.

Their younger son's death at 42 years old was the result of his involvement with drugs. His brother never could get his life back together. He is having to live a different lifestyle from how he grew up. It is hard to imagine seeing him now compared to how he was growing up. It was a lesson that teaches you not to envy someone for what they have and how they are living. We are to be thankful for what we have; because the envy turned into sadness for the family.

To the left of us was a family with two daughters. The youngest daughter and I were friends. I remember many nights we would stand outside and talk until late. She moved to Rochester, New York, in her early twenties and made it her home. Her sister was my son's godmother.

Then there was a lady who was living with her husband across the street. She was a stout woman who always sat on her front porch, passing the time away. My sister and I would do all we could to avoid passing her house. The thing we'd dislike the most was when she would ask to suck on our julep. She would say, "Come here, honey, let me taste your julep." Afterward, my sister and I would throw it away. She'd do it because she knew we would not want it anymore, hoping we would give it to her and we did a few times. She could have given us the money to buy her one, but she preferred to lick on our julep. It was not nice for her to take advantage of children. Others said she would beg for their food.

When her husband passed away, she moved back to her hometown. She sold her home to the grandparents next-door who were raising their five grandchildren.

Those grandparents, after the death of their daughter, displayed selfless devotion. It takes a lot to take on the role and responsibility of raising five grandchildren. Their grandparents were to be commended. You would think the odds would have been against those kids, but they were all smart and intelligent and became successful. The oldest brother, after serving in the military, worked for the State.

The brother younger than him overcame his drug addiction and dedicated his life to helping others who struggled with the same dependency. He is the Founder, President, and CEO of his health services organization that provides supportive transitional housing for adult males and females seeking recovery from alcohol or other drug abuse. God allowed his purpose for life to be manifested through his addiction. He had to go through seasons of that drug dependency to fulfill God's bigger picture for him. It was God's will for him to help others heal who are struggling with drug addictions. *To every thing, there is a season and a time to every purpose under the heaven*: (Eccles. 3:1 KJV).

Their sister, who was a close friend and a sweet person, passed away in 2018 after a car accident. After graduating high school, they offered her a scholarship to attend Harvard University. With her grandmother's illness, she opted to remain close to their home and eventually graduated from the University of South Florida. She and her husband were both ministers. The other sister, who was my classmate, according to her obituary, passed away in 2013. She served in the US Army and the youngest brother is a lead associate at a company.

Loved going to the playground

Behind where we lived was The Palmetto Youth Center, founded in 1957; its goal was to provide a positive atmosphere for youth. There were always some activities going on like softball, baseball, football, or basketball games. It was a place for kids and teenagers to go. They would also use the building for other community functions. On the weekends, they sometimes would have a dance, and people would come from different places. You had to pay to attend the dance. We would look forward to going and hanging out with friends. There was also a playground where kids would play.

There was a boy whose grandparents lived in the neighborhood, and he would come to visit them from Ocala, Fl. They lived around the corner from us. I remember his grandmother worked at this restaurant and would bring home the best-tasting biscuits. She would also make them, and they were yummy. His aunt and I were friends, and she would sneak me a biscuit.

I always loved going to the playground until this one day. Having fun and swinging on the swings. I had stopped swinging and was just sitting. This boy was always very mean. He and I began exchanging words.

He said, "I'm going to hit you with this swing." It was one of those swings made with thick chains and a wooden seat. I said, "I bet you won't hit me with that swing," and before getting the words out, he let the swing go. All I could recall was seeing a flash, and to this day, it left a scar on my left eye, right on my eyebrow. I didn't think he would let that swing go, but he did. Crying, with blood gushing everywhere, I ran toward home.

Many years later, I was honored when his family trusted me to sell their family home as a realtor. I truly thanked them for giving me the opportunity.

Young entrepreneur

I was a young entrepreneur and would earn money as a young girl by walking around the neighborhood, picking up empty soda bottles along the road and out of the ditch, and saving them. My mother would take me to the store to purchase a bottle crate. Once I filled the wooden boxes with twenty-four empty bottles, I would take them to the store, get paid for the deposits on the bottles, and get the money back for the crate. This allowed me to make a little money for myself as a child. Some people would be ashamed of picking up empty bottles, but it was a way for me to make money, and I was thankful.

Apologize and ask for forgiveness

In sixth grade, I got into a scuffle with a classmate. When we started, the teacher or someone pulled my hands together behind my back, and she just went for my face. What caused it was that she had her head down on the desk, and out of concern for her, I asked her what was wrong; I guess she did not want me talking to her, so she jumped out of her seat and started fighting me. I did not expect her to react in that manner. Today, we are cordial with one another. She sends me their church-recorded services on Messenger. I enjoy the pastor; he is awesome when I would watch his services.

There was another incident in the sixth grade with a classmate. I won't go into details because the memory of it hurts me when I think about it. God led me some years back as an adult to call her to apologize and ask for her forgiveness. She was such a sweet person and still is. What took place was being urged by peer pressure. I am so proud of whom she has become. She has a (Ph.D.) in theology and philosophy. And is now a university professor, chaplain, and senior pastor of her church.

Restaurant days

When reflecting, my mother and father had separated, and I was dealing with anger. I was very mean and rebellious. Those were tough years for me. It was in 1970 when my life started changing, and not for the good. After my mom and dad separated, I started hanging out at the restaurant my mother owned. I remember my father being there in the beginning. Therefore, they must have separated and divorced during her years at her business. While there, I would hang out at friends' houses near the restaurant. Sometimes, I'd get money out of my mom's money box, which she used as a cash register, and catch the downtown city bus to go shopping.

This friend, we had the same first and last name before I changed mine to my dad's last name. Her father may have been White, and she may have told me he was. My friend was a pretty girl. She had this cute little sausage dog named Tuggy and he had a long nose, and she had a long nose. I'd tease her and tell her she looked like Tuggy. She would laugh. She contacted me a few years ago, and the first thing from her mouth was, "I still know how to spell Czechoslovakia." I taught her how to spell it. Practicing spelling hard words used to be my thing, but not anymore.

I met many people while hanging out at my mother's restaurant. This young lady that lived in the back of the restaurant taught me how to sew. She taught me everything one needed to know to sew pretty much anything. So, I started spending a lot of time in fabric stores buying patterns and fabric.

Making pantsuits, short sets, dresses, skirts, costumes, curtains, and you name it. Surprising myself, I made this white coat for this guy and did not think I could have made a coat that nice. Getting too many requests for sewing made me decide to stop. Also, times changed, and it was cheaper to buy your clothes than the cost of making them. If you were looking for a special outfit, you could not find in the stores, you might be okay with paying the price to have someone make it.

Young and naïve

Anyway, a guy, years older than me, lived with his parents in the back of the restaurant. I was a young girl and had a crush on him. He'd sometimes come over and sit with me on the bench outside in front of the restaurant. One evening, I was not where I needed to be, so my mother closed her restaurant and left for home. It was getting dark, and this guy offered to walk me home. We were walking down the railroad tracks. This must have happened in March 1970. I was a 13-year-old little girl. He was told, "No." It must have been in April when I missed my cycle. I was taken advantage of and got pregnant, by this guy who manipulated my being naïve.

My mother, being a God-fearing woman, did not believe in abortions. Being a child myself, I did not need a child, but on December 1, 1971, at 7:40 a.m., my son was born. Everything has its time. *A time to be born*, (Eccles. 3:2a KJV). I was a child with a child. For years, I had so much bitterness, anger, and resentment. You didn't quite know what those feelings were about. My childhood had been taken away. I have since learned that everything has its time. Everything has its purpose. I believe it was a part of the plan God had for my life.

Being young and naïve, I suppose it was me trying to fill a void after the breakup between my mother and father. I woke up one morning, and the feelings I thought I had for my son's father were gone. My son was a few months old. His father begged me not to end the relationship, but it was over. It was nothing but infatuation. A father in the home is so vital in a young girl's life. His absence in the house can be detrimental to his child's well-being.

One day, my son's father had been riding in a car with friends, and they were playing with a gun. One of his friends shot him in the head. The doctors weren't able to remove the bullet because it could have paralyzed him. He continued to live for years, but it was affecting him. He was a great artist. When he graduated high school, they offered him a full scholarship to attend Ringling School of Arts in Sarasota, Fl. Unfortunately, he wasn't able to take advantage of it after his accident.

His family moved to Tampa, Florida. According to his family, he would go downtown Tampa to the park where he would draw. If someone wanted their picture drawn, they would sit, and he would draw a picture of them. It was how he made a living for himself. When his son grew up, he also had those artistic abilities.

Some memories I had with him

We would take a shortcut to get to my grandmother's house. My son's father and I were walking through that shortcut one night, and he hit me. I can't recall why. But, it was his first and last time hitting me. My brother, who lived with my grandmother, may have seen my son's father hit me but kept walking and would not say anything. He and his brothers were always getting into fights. He punched this boy in the cafeteria in high school in 1971, which started a riot. I probably would have been in an abusive relationship. God knows what is best for us; He can see much further ahead than we can. God knew he was not the right one for me.

One evening, my mother and I left her restaurant and headed home. We saw my son's father walking towards the bridge that takes you to the next town. He was trying to hitchhike a ride there. During those days, that's what guys would do. Most of the guys did not own cars, so they hitched a ride where they needed to go. I knew he was heading to see his girlfriend because someone had told me he had one that lived there. So, I asked my mom to give him a ride because it was my way of letting him know I knew where he was going. He got in the car, and we gave him a ride. I thought it was funny, but it wasn't very comfortable.

My teenage years were shattered

During this time, my dad was not taking any part in my life. He and my mom had separated. During their separation, I remember I went with my mother to the grove where he picked fruit. She wanted to talk to him about not paying the child support he was court-ordered to pay.

He only had to pay her twenty dollars a month. It was ten dollars for me and ten dollars for my sister. I recalled the fact that he would only pay her ten dollars. It never dawned that he didn't want to pay the other ten dollars because he either did not believe I was his child or knew I was not his child. I believed he was my father because no one ever said anything different. Indeed, the suspicions were there because there was just no resemblance.

My teenage years growing up like normal teenagers were shattering. My dad was no longer living with us; now, I have a child. I tried returning to high school but felt I was no longer accepted into the mainstream. I was being looked down upon for having a baby, and I had to deal with guilt and

21

shame. You had those stereotypes. People thought they were better than you. I ended up missing out on a lot because I was being excluded from everything. You end up getting forgotten about. Even now, you are not being included in class reunions, etc.

Being determined, the same year my classmates graduated in 1975, I received my high school diploma. By attending night school and adult vocational school, the drive was there not to let having a baby hold me back. Life continued to move forward.

Chapter Two

Siblings

My oldest brother

An honor student throughout his school years, my oldest brother was always quiet and easygoing. He graduated at 17 and went into the military, the Air Force. Before that, he was living in Boston with relatives.

I'm not sure if my brother was married before joining the military because I have little memory of him being in the house with us. He's been married and divorced a few times. When he was in the military, he took me to visit him and his family. They had stationed him in Panama City, Florida, and he lived on base in military housing. After being there for a few days, I started missing my mother and being away. So, it was time for me to go back home to my mom.

I appreciated my oldest brother for allowing me to come and visit. He loved this famous singing group and would play this one song while I was there that would make me cry. A sentence from the lyrics told me; you better go back home where you belong. He'd make fun of me because he knew I was ready to go home. He loved his music and had plenty of albums.

When I was twelve, he and his best friend took me to the FAMU game in Tallahassee, Florida. It was a long ride, but I had a chance as a pre-teen to travel with him to Tallahassee and watch that outstanding band with their fantastic performance. I never forgot that. It meant so much to me for my oldest brother to take me to the game with him and his best friend. My brother also loved to dress. He learned how to sew and would make some of his pants and did an excellent job.

He and his current wife have been married for 45 years. She has always been a pleasant person. They have two children together, and he has a stepson. He also had a son with his first wife named after him, who passed away on August 15, 2015. Like his dad, he served in the military. The son he and his current wife had together is working on his graduate degree and is teaching at a local school. His daughter has her bachelor's degree and also teaches at a local school.

My brother also has a daughter he had out of wedlock and I admire her because she has five boys that she practically raised by herself until she married later the father of her youngest son. While raising those boys, she received her master's degree and is a licensed mental health counselor. Her sons are now young men doing well in life except for one who got into trouble.

Her youngest son completed high school and graduated with a 4.0-grade point average, and received a scholarship to college for academics and sports. He plays basketball. My brother's grandson, by him and his wife's son, completed high school and will attend college on a football scholarship.

My brother retired from the local Juvenile Detention Center in an administrative role and continues to work after he retired.

My second-oldest brother
A miracle from God

I was told, my second oldest brother was born with veiling over his face. Being born with a veil over your face means God has a spiritual purpose for you. On a Tuesday night, when he was six years old, he had rheumatic fever and a hole in his heart, according to him. In the middle of the night, he started hemorrhaging from the nose. Our mother, grandmother, and aunt took him to the hospital. They had to wait a long time before the doctor came in and looked at him. After seeing him, the doctor told them to take him home; he would be deceased by the end of the week.

As they were going back home, driving across the bridge, my mom, grandmother, and aunt were whispering, trying to decide how to tell him he was going to die. He told his grandmother to call the pastor and have him come and pray for him, and he would be all right. I was told he had not walked in over a month. The following Sunday after church, the pastor came to the house. My grandmother and mother brought my brother out of the room and set him in a chair in the living room.

After the pastor prayed for him, he stood up, stumbled twice, and walked out of the house. He walked to my aunt's house, where our grandpapa was visiting, to get him a dollar. He hasn't been sick since, and it has been close to 70 years. His faith in God healed him. They experienced a miracle to show all those around them God's healing power, and for my brother to share with others his testimony. God is a healing God and wants to heal us if we have faith and believe.

Three months later, my brother got saved and preached his first sermon at seven years old. The speech addressed the Gospel of John, 15th Chapter: True Vine. At nine years old, he served as assistant pastor and assistant secretary, as was told to me.

During my teenage years, he was not around much. When he was, when I would try to clean up their room, he would get furious and throw his shoes at me. My brothers would have shoes and clothes scattered everywhere. They had a problem with their younger sister coming into their bedroom and cleaning up. They viewed it as me being nosey.

He was asked to leave the church

He ended up getting a girl pregnant when he was 16 years old, and because of it, he was told to leave the church. He became the father of a daughter. The mother had another child, and he later learned she was his daughter. She looks more like him than the first daughter. They both have earned their master's degrees. One is a licensed clinical therapist, and the other is a licensed mental health counselor.

When he graduated high school in 1970, he was the first black to make the Hall of Fame for Academics and Sports. He also graduated with several other honors. After receiving a full academic scholarship to attend the University of Florida in Gainesville, he moved to live on campus there. Once attending, he started partying, doing many things, and having a good time. He said he would sign up for classes and not attend them. When it was time to take a test; he would go to class; take it and pass.

He married his high school sweetheart, and they had two children together. They named their son after him. Their son lived with my aunt until he was four years old while his parents were in college. After my aunt passed away, they lived in her home for a while. Their son and our son played and hung out together because they were the same age. I will never forget when I smoked cigarettes for a short period when I was younger; he told me, "Auntie, you don't look right smoking." That comment from him remained on my mind and helped me to stop smoking.

My brother and his wife later purchased a home and moved to Bradenton. They had a daughter while living there. She was born a year before our daughter and they grew up together. We lived around the corner from each other until they moved to Gainesville. We made many trips back and forth from Gainesville to their home.

Their son attended FAMU in Tallahassee, Florida. He earned a bachelor's degree in business administration. While there, he started the Phat Cat Players; being known for their CD, "Make It Phat Baby," his hit, "Sundress," released in 1999. With that deep voice, women all over the country wanted to know who "Cocoa Brown" was. His alter ego's name is "Coco Brown." A poet with a deep voice. He has also ventured into the film industry.

In Tyler Perry's 2006 film, "Madea's Family Reunion," when Frankie and Vanessa walked into the Jazz Club, he was finishing up a spoken word "poem," Frankie told Vanessa, "I told you he was good." As the "MC," he said, "What I want yawl to do now, crowd, is put your hands together for Frankie and Vanessa." Frankie and Vanessa walk up to the stage; Vanessa does a spoken word "poem" while Frankie draws her picture. When they are completed, as the "MC," he says, "We are all family here; you all show them some love, please." He continues to pursue ventures.

He also has another daughter born out of wedlock who has earned several degrees and doing well for herself. He fathered five children in total and has grandchildren. One of his grandkids has finished college and is now teaching, but pursuing his master's degree. Another graduated with a bachelor's in computer engineering and his sister is in school to get a nursing degree like her grandmother. Another granddaughter by his son graduated from Howard University in Washington, D.C.

Rededicated his life

During the years, life continued to have its way with my brother. He had not attended church since being put out for getting his daughter's mother pregnant at 16. When his life started falling apart, he rededicated his life to Christ while living in Gainesville.

He and his first wife divorced. They both later remarried, but she passed away on November 26, 2015. People had nothing but kind words to say about her. Even though they had divorced, I still looked at her as my sister-in-law.

He admits he has made many mistakes in his life. Being very knowledgeable, everyone had high expectations of him. It bothers him that he failed his first marriage. He loved his family. He has been married several times since, but those marriages did not work out.

He earned a degree in Theology and in 1998, he and his second wife started a church. The church was prospering, but as years went on, the membership dwindled. The church had to close its doors in 2019.

He is an excellent teacher of the word of God and knows the Bible, but probably needs to work out some things within like we all do.

He's always jovial, and some people do not know how to handle his personality. He is a good man who believes God has called him.

My Third oldest brother

The Instigator

My brother, three years older, always tried to get me in trouble. He was an instigator and would tell my grandmother everything I would do. He would stay at her house most of the time.

One time he caught me taking mulberries from a neighbor's tree. My mind told me when I looked up and saw that he was standing at my grandmother's door, that he would go back and tell her. I saw him easing his foot back into the house, just knowing he would get me in trouble. My grandmother had him get a switch from the tree in her yard. She had me running around the bed, trying to get away. The rest is history.

He was my grandmother's favorite of my mother's children. Therefore, he spent most of his time around her. Being like a son to her, my grandmother spoiled him. Some say that you should never spoil a boy because he will expect it from every woman. This has been the case with him. Women would always comment and say, "He is one good-looking, tall, dark-skinned man." It was used to his advantage and not in a good way. Dressing up from head to toe is who he is. He is a sharp dresser and loves his wide-brim hats.

Inferiority

Because his skin is darker than the rest of his siblings, he always considered himself inferior. Children in school were mean and picked on him because of his darker complexion. It bothered him and affected his self-esteem. As a result of that, he ended up dropping out of high school. He always felt he was not as intelligent as his brothers. But the fact is, he is just as smart, he just doesn't have confidence in himself. Therefore, he grew up having more street smarts.

We were talking one day, and he told me about a time when he had stopped to visit one of our neighbor friends, whom many envied in our neighborhood. It was at another house owned by the family, but his friend lived in that home with his wife. He said, the wife answered the door and would not invite him in. I felt so bad when my brother shared that with me. It bothered him. He believed she thought he was beneath them. He grew up next door to this neighbor friend, but his wife thought he was not good enough to be invited into their home. I do not want to try and interpret that situation, because she may have had her reasons, but we should never try to make someone feel inferior no matter who they are.

Most of my brother's close friends and associates have passed away. He is still living, and I know it's those prayers that went up from his mother and grandmother. He and I have been very close, and because of his lack of education, I assist him with things he doesn't understand.

On another note, both my brother's wives lived in my grandmother's house with him during their marriage. His first wife moved away to Connecticut with his daughter and filed for a divorce. He later remarried, and they divorced. Afterward, he discovered he and his first wife had never divorced. He knew she had applied for it and thought he was a single man. He has several children born out of wedlock, with whom he is not close. A couple of them the family has met, and others we have not. His daughter as an adult is doing well for herself while living in Connecticut. One of his sons lives in Texas and is married and has three beautiful children. He has earned a two-year degree.

Before my grandmother passed away, according to my brother, she informed him she was leaving her house to her son, our uncle, because it was what his father wanted when they built the house together. She told him he could continue living there as long as needed. My grandmother also told him her son, his uncle, needed help after being in the military. She knew the military had affected him mentally and wanted to ensure her son had the house his father built for them to live in once she passed on.

Property taxes

When my brother and his second wife lived in the house, they would not pay the property taxes nor would they do anything to repair it. I'd been paying the delinquent taxes yearly and was expecting to be reimbursed, but was not. So, maybe it was my brother's conversation with his grandmother about the house belonging to his uncle that he refused to invest money into it. Whatever the case may be, it became apparent that his wife, while residing there was saving her money. When she separated from him in 2003, she moved into her own home she was purchasing.

In Florida, if you do not pay your property taxes and they become delinquent, the tax collector will hold a tax certificate sale. The person who purchases the tax certificate can collect your outstanding debt plus interest. In addition, the tax collector will sell the home at a public tax deed sale if you, the homeowner, or whoever does not pay the past-due amounts.

Based on our grandmother's property taxes on her home not being paid and going delinquent, the above situation could have occurred because no one offered to help me make the overdue payments.

Her property could have gone to someone for the outstanding tax amounts plus interest. The property became estate property when she passed away because she did not have a will. Therefore, it was going to need to be probated.

I contacted an attorney, and because of six siblings, and my uncle's sons, it would have been costly to probate the property. The value of the property would not have been worth it. The attorney advised me to have all my siblings agree to sign their portion of the property over to me by signing a Simple Fee Deed. This way, they would no longer have ownership of the property. My uncle's sons who lived in New York were sent letters by the attorney but never responded. I'd later learned, it was their property based on what my grandmother told my brother.

After the attorney mailed them letters and received no response, the legal notice was posted in the newspaper in the county where they lived. If they did not respond within a certain period, that ended it. They never responded. I became the official owner of the property once all my siblings, simple Fee deeds, were recorded.

The property was sold in February 2003 for the land. The next step could have been letting it get sold on the courthouse steps to the highest bidder for the delinquent fees and interest. We know these situations can create different feelings for different family members. To property owners, handle your business and make out a will. Do not speak about whom you want your property to pass on to when you are deceased. Get it in writing to avoid these types of situations.

My Fourth Oldest brother

My brother, two years older than I spent much of his time at our grandaunt's house. He was one of her favorite grandnephews. The reason he spent most of his time at her house was that he had somewhat of a better living while being around her. She did not have any children. She used to work at this little neighborhood store and she would run the store because she and the owner were close. She would allow my brother who was a teenager to work behind the counter. This is where he met his teenage sweetheart. She also worked there and lived not far from us.

Joined the military

He would also help his mother in her restaurant. While working in the restaurant, he made a conscious decision that whoever he married, would never have to go through what he witnessed his mother endure. His girlfriend became pregnant, and he dropped out of high school. Before dropping out of high school, he was an honor student. He and his girlfriend got married and have been together for almost 50 years if not fifty.

He signed up and went into the military in the early seventies. While in the military, he completed his high school education. My mother received a letter from the military informing her that my brother had been selected as the 3785th Field Training Wing FTD Flight Supervisor for 1988. It was an honor of distinction, quote, "he richly earned," as stated in the letter. In 1988, he received a Bachelor of Professional Aeronautics Degree from Embry-Riddle Aeronautical University in Daytona Beach, Florida.

Due to them being in the military, they were not around. Madrid, Spain is one of the many places they had been stationed. The other places they have lived and visited are too many to remember.

Stationed in Panama City, Florida, my memory as a teenager, my mother had given him her Oldsmobile cutlass when she got a new car. He passed down the Oldsmobile cutlass to me when he purchased a new vehicle. My brother, three years older, drove to Panama City with me to drive the car back home to Bradenton. I was so happy to get that car. It meant so much to me.

Presidential award ceremony

After serving 20 years in the Air Force, my brother retired in 1994. We were told it takes someone 20 years to get the stripe he had when he retired. In 10 years, he had earned it. He, his wife, and younger son lived with us in our home for several months in Bradenton until they were situated after he retired from the military. He now has a government job with enormous responsibilities. At a Presidential Award Ceremony in Washington, D.C., held in 2012, he was one of the Meritorious Executive Rank Award recipients for sustained accomplishments for the fiscal year 2011. It was an event where the President of the United States recognized an elite group of career senior executives.

My sister-in-law has always had a spirit of giving. She has been in our lives for a long time. We seem to butt heads a lot. Therefore, our relationship gets testy. However, she and my other sister-in-law, my husband's sister, were the only family members to allow me as a realtor to receive a commission in a real estate transaction. I will always be grateful to them both for their act of kindness. My brother and his wife raised three children. Their oldest son attended the University of

Notre Dame College, one of the top universities in the world. He was drafted in the 3rd round in 1994 by the San Diego Chargers and played professional football from 1994 to 1998.

He played for The Philadelphia Eagles in the National Football League in 1997. A cornerback was his position. Ironically, he did not play many sports when he was younger. My son and nephew (whose alter ego is Coco Brown) would be outside playing sports; he would be inside on the floor reading an encyclopedia. He decided to give up playing professional football early because of his interest in education. Currently, he is an executive director of secondary education for the local school board.

His younger son attended a local high school and played football as a cornerback. He was a three-year starter at cornerback for Georgia Tech College in Atlanta, Georgia. His dream was to play in the NFL like his brother. He is now a principal at a local middle school academy. Their daughter, with several degrees, is a guidance counselor at a local school. They are all married, have children in college or have completed college, are in high school, middle or elementary school, and doing great things.

My baby sister

My sister is four years younger, the baby sister. She was a beautiful baby and a pretty girl. I always had to hear that. She looks just like our dad. It is as if he gave birth to her by himself. He is definitely her father. Even though we supposedly share the same dad, my sister and I do not look anything alike, and neither does she have much resemblance to our mother. My sister has a much lighter complexion; my color is much darker and I am pretty sure curiosity had folks asking, was he, my biological father?

I always believed my sister could get away with anything because she was the youngest. She never had to experience the name-calling from our brothers as they treated me because they were older and had left the house. With her skin complexion and being pretty as she was, they would not have anyway. They have always treated her differently.

Got away with everything

Growing up, I was doing most of everything that was getting done around the house. There was always an excuse for why she could get away with things. It caused me to have much resentment toward her. Growing up, she would receive the brunt of my meanness because she always got her way. She still demands to have her way and when she does not get it, she gets upset.

When we were young, we worked on a program called NYC during the summer. You had to qualify, and the program was to help students learn on-the-job training. There had to be employers willing to work with the program to hire the students during the summer months. My sister would get paid, go to the mall, and come home with a couple of dollars. I would hand my paycheck over to my mom. She just got away with everything.

My sister was always different. One time, we had to look for her when she was little; maybe around ten years old, give or take. We could not find her. When they found her, she was at this neighborhood store with a shopping cart, and as I can recall, there were plenty of cans of pork and beans in the cart.

Sleepwalking

She would also sleepwalk. One night my mother or someone in the house woke up and the door was wide open. My sister was sleepwalking and walked around the corner to my grandmother's house, and they found her sitting on the steps. It was around one or two o'clock in the morning. Being bold and not afraid of anything describes her even now. She was always a happy child. She loved playing sports and had lots of friends when she was younger. An optimistic person she has always been with just a beautiful spirit. She doesn't hold grudges and has always had a thing for helping others.

At a young age, she got pregnant and gave birth to a daughter. It was not a long-term relationship between her and her baby's father. He passed away when his daughter was small. While still young, she married a guy and gave birth to two sons. She divorced him because of infidelity and having too many outside children during their marriage. She has married again twice and divorced.

Nine lives

My sister was involved in an accident years ago with injuries that brought Multiple Sclerosis to the surface. She was told it had been lying dormant until the accident. Being the person she is, she lets nothing get her down. We tell her she has nine lives like a cat. We know it has been those prayers sent up by our mother and grandmother. She has survived breast cancer and keeps it moving; nothing stops her. God is good, He will never leave or forsake us. A persistent and determined person she

43

is. We admire her for her perseverance and her strong will. Throughout her life, when meeting someone, she would always call them her friends. I would tell her repeatedly that those people were not her friends. She kept having to find it out for herself.

She loves cooking. She and her third husband owned a restaurant for a while. Bringing the family together for family gatherings is something she loves to do. It allows her to cook and be around her family. They are always having gatherings to bring their family together, and because she loves being around people. She has many grandchildren and raised one of her grandsons. Her children are doing well in life and they are there for their mother.

Called names and made fun of

Before my sister was born, being raised with four brothers was not always easy. My brothers, except the oldest, would call me names like; bald head, skinny witch, flat butt, little legs, and other ugly names as a child. One brother would tell me that baking soda makes things rise, and if I would eat baking soda, maybe my butt will rise.

One reminded me that someone in the family would say, look at her running around the house looking like this bird with a long neck and tiny legs. He could not figure out the name of the bird he was trying to say. It shocked me that the person would say that about me. My brothers did not know at the time those things they were saying about me would affect me throughout my life. They were being teenagers.

Because of my tiny ankles, I was always called skinny legs. They are running legs, muscled at the top and small at the bottom. Later in life, I realized those demeaning things being said to me when I was young caused me to be self-conscious and insecure. It made me not want to be around people. I always stood back within a crowd. I will admit I called them names back. I had to defend myself.

Thanks to my second oldest brother, after I was an adult advised me to wear everything above my knees or at my knees. This way, my full legs would show instead of what I'm wearing, stopping between the muscle of my legs and my tiny ankles. It made a difference in showing my full legs. I indeed thanked him for that advice.

One day as a teenager, while standing outside talking with my neighbor friend that lived across the street, my mother was coming from my grandmother's house and walked past us. I told my friend, "Look at my mama's muscle in her legs." My mother said nothing to me then, but when I got home, I discovered her self-consciousness about her legs. She was very upset with me and I learned not to do that again.

Chapter Three

My Mother

My mother was married and divorced twice before marrying my dad. She had been married to my two oldest brother's father. For a short time, she had been married to someone else. She and my dad were married in March 1958. So, when they were married, my mother already had four kids. Then I was born, and my sister was born four years later. I was the first girl born. I was told we would have had two more sisters because my mother had a miscarriage carrying twins. And I've been told all my life that I looked like my mother.

Growing up, my mother was not a mother that showed much affection, but we knew she loved us. She showed us her love through her hard work and providing for us. She was a God-fearing woman and did her best to serve God. When we were young, she would take my sister and me to church. I can't recall my brothers being there; they were older. My mother would be very involved in the church, teaching Sunday school and singing in the choir. I was told our mother had gone to Detroit to make a record but had to come back home. My sister and I would also sing in the choir.

My mother used to pay a lady to come to the house to teach me and my sister music lessons until the lady told her to stop wasting her money. The piano was there, just beautifying the living room. What's sad is that we did not take advantage of it and we both regretted it later.

Her restaurant

She was a hard-working woman for as long as I can remember. She loved cooking and worked in several restaurants throughout Manatee County. Then in 1969 or 1970, she opened her own business. A restaurant on Tenth Street in Palmetto.

During that time, many black businesses were on that street. There was a black-owned dry cleaners attached next door to her restaurant. Across the street was a black-owned barber shop on the corner; next to it was a black-owned taxi stand; down the road from the taxi stand heading west was a black club on the corner; across from it was a black-owned liquor store and club. There was also a bar, a grocery store, and a pool hall on the north side of the street. Across from them on the south side was another black-owned barbershop. Now those black businesses no longer exist along Tenth Street in Palmetto.

My mother did very well in the restaurant, but it was a lot of hard work. It was a soul food restaurant. She would sell dinners like fried chicken, pork chops, chitterlings, stew beef, short ribs, and you name it. Also, hamburgers and fries she would sell, and those hamburgers were the bum. It was the way she buttered the buns and put them on the grill. People loved her food. She was an excellent cook.

The setup inside was about five or six sit-down tables and chairs. A counter with stools where you could sit and eat. It extended in a curve shape with a glass counter filled with honey buns, chips, candy, sour pickles, spicy sausages, etc. A jukebox inside for customers to listen to music if desired. Someone would put a quarter in the jukebox and play a record of their choice. To this day, when I hear the records customers used to play in the restaurant, it brings back many memories. They would lift my mood and make me think of my mother. Also, if I am feeling a little down and I happen to hear one of those old songs, it makes me feel much better.

Sometimes, it was difficult for her to get reliable help in her restaurant. My brother, two years older, would come to help by washing the dishes and doing whatever he could to help her after school. My mother would work so hard. One evening, my mother was tired and was trying to close up for the evening. My dad kept letting customers come in the door. So, my brother stood up to my dad. He told him, "Don't you let another customer come through that door. Can't you see my mother is tired?" Working so hard would wear my mother out.

Therefore, she felt like my dad could watch her work herself to death. They had their struggles, and my mother was getting extremely tired. I remember the pastor coming over one day to pray for her, and she was crying and crying and could not stop. I don't remember my dad being at the house when that took place.

An outstanding mother

My parents separated during the early 70s and my dad did not want the separation. He took it very hard. After the separation, my mother became more independent. She already knew how to drive; she purchased herself a brand new Oldsmobile Cutlass. They divorced in November 1972. My mother remarried the same year while my dad remarried in June 1973.

I really never knew what caused them to divorce, but when my dad was in the rehabilitation center, he admitted to me when I asked him whether it was true about him and this person while married to my mom. He told me how it happened and how one thing led to another. I was surprised to find that out. When he was with my mother, he always denied it. Whether my mom and dad were still living together or separated when it happened, I can't recall.

My mother had her faults, as we all do; none of us are perfect. I know she was a very extravagant woman. She loved the best, and she loved shopping. My mother would go to the store and come home with bags of items for my sister and me. She would shop at stores that most people could not afford to shop in those days. She wore expensive clothing and would buy them for us. We always had the best. She would dress us all in fine clothing even though she had six children.

My mother was also competitive. One day, the next-door neighbor, whom many envied, had gotten a new Cadillac car which was gray. As mentioned, the neighbors would exchange Cadillac cars every two or three years. So, my mother had a beautiful yellow Cadillac. In conversation, I stated how pretty the neighbor's car was with the gray color. My mother did not have her car very long, but because I complimented the neighbor's vehicle, she traded her new yellow one for gray. There was nothing wrong with her yellow Cadillac; it was beautiful. I should have kept my mouth closed.

Despite that, my mother was a strong, independent, loving, intelligent, determined, and beautiful-spirited woman. She worked hard to have the things she desired. She was always smiling, saying kind words, and encouraging others. She would always display a sweet spirit. She loved giving and helping others therefore, she used to collect shoes and clothing from stores after convincing the store managers to make donations to her to give to the needy.

My mother believed in the power of prayer. Therefore, when I would go through difficulties, she would always tell me to pray. When going through anxiety, she would advise me to continue to say,

"Lord, I praise you for your peace," and I would do that along with thanking God for everything. Up to this day, it has brought me through.

One day, I was driving home and it was raining. Approaching a red light at 1st Street and 13th Avenue East in Bradenton, I began to slightly put my foot on the brakes, when my car spent around. A semi-truck had to run off the road onto the field of a nearby school to keep from hitting my car. Being so shaken up, all I could do was cry and thank God for stopping that truck from hitting me from behind. That should have been the death of me on that day. But, God....

Walking through the door, after making it home, my son, who was around six years old, came running to me, wrapped his arms around my legs, and said, "Mama, grandma was praying for you." Because it was raining, she must have felt danger for me, and she was praying for my safety. Her prayers saved my life and my son verified that. Thank you, God. My mother was a praying woman who taught me to do the same.

Nobody could ever say that my mother would speak down to her children. She would always encourage us. Women envied her because of what she had. Growing up, letting friends or people use or take advantage of her would make me so angry. She was always so pleasant and giving, and it seemed they never returned it. I would ask her, "Mama, why do you keep buying gifts for those people, and they don't do it for you?" She always told me, "You kill them with kindness, darling." Her other favorite saying was, "Treat people how you want to be treated." She was a loving mother to all of her children and grandchildren.

An excellent cook

She was a skilled cook, and the family enjoyed her cooking. During the holidays, she would always cook a big dinner for us. You can look forward to Christmas and Thanksgiving, having ham, turkey, chitterlings, yams, collard greens, macaroni and cheese, rice, and cornbread. For desserts, it would always be chocolate and coconut cakes, apple pies, pecan and sweet potato pies, nuts, and holiday candy.

Even though my mom always made delicious desserts, she did not like it when I would comment on how good my grandma's pound cake tasted. It's her mother, and making pound cakes was her mother's specialty. My mother did not make a pound cake that often, but she was very competitive in cooking. She wrote a cookbook before she

passed, but getting it published never happened.
Somehow it was misplaced between her moving.

When she lived in Tampa, she worked for
MacDill Air Force Base in their kitchen and was
recognized and received an award for Sustained
Superior Performance. It is an award for exceptional
performance within two years for regular job duties
that result in the efficiency of the State government.

My mother sought other jobs outside of
cooking at one time, and she attended school for
something in the medical field. For a few years, she
worked at the local health department. She moved
to Gainesville with my second oldest brother and
his family sometime between 1987 and 1991. She
then moved back to Bradenton and lived with my
husband and me for a short while. Also, years ago,
she spent some time with my brother, two years
older, and his wife in Tampa.

At one point, my husband and I, with my
mother, opened a little restaurant called Barbeque
Ribs and Things in Palmetto. We sold dinners,
barbeque sandwiches, shrimp baskets, hamburgers,
cheeseburgers, and fries. My third oldest brother
helped by sometimes cooking the ribs and working
the counter. We were doing well for me to attend

school, work full time, and work in the restaurant when it was opened.

The decline of her health

During this time was when my mother began experiencing health issues. We closed the restaurant after about a year and a half because she often became fatigued. After living with us for a little while, she wanted to be on her own again.

I contacted a lady who lived in Palmetto, whom people would say, was a religious fanatic because she had bible scriptures written all over her car. I had much respect for this lady and her beliefs. It was in my heart to contact her to pray for my mother to find an affordable place to live. Two weeks after I reached out to her for prayer, a door opened for my mother to move into an apartment. They accepted her into an apartment complex in Bradenton. God worked it out because prayer changes things.

This was a significant change for my mother. She had left behind a beautiful home because of my stepfather's infidelity. Before my stepfather became out of control about his affair, they had added additions to the house. They added a large main bedroom and a patio with a garden next to the large

family room. She was growing beautiful rosebushes
in her garden. A mural was put up in her living
room. Again, it was a beautiful home. However, she
lost it to foreclosure after moving to another town.

What my mother was going through was
devastating and traumatic. She should not have had
to go through what she experienced at her age. It
had to be very stressful. She had been used to living
a different lifestyle most of her life.

All of this was taking a toll on her health. She
had to get blood transfusions, and doctors could not
determine where her blood was going. One day at
the end of 1993 or 1994, she stumped her toe on her
coffee table and it wouldn't heal. This led to her toe
being amputated. It was because of diabetic
neuropathy. Her kidneys started shutting down, and
she began having to have dialysis treatments, which
she could do at home for a while. So, she later
started going to the dialysis center. She would still
continue to encourage others, no matter how sick
she was.

Then, after her toe amputation, they ended up
removing one of her legs. She went from the
hospital to a rehabilitation facility. Unable to take
care of her because of having to work and help
provide for the family, I began living with regrets.

My mother gave up after having her leg amputated and the thought of being in a facility. She never wanted to be a burden on anyone. She had always been so independent. It hurts my heart to think about how she suffered after having so much love to give to her family and others.

During her last days, someone mentioned to me that sometimes you have to tell your loved ones that are suffering and holding on that it's ok if they want to go. Many times they are holding on thinking the loved ones they are leaving behind needs them. It was the hardest thing for me, but I told her, "Mama if you are ready to go, it is ok." She just stared in a daze. I asked her, "Mama, did you hear me?" With a tear rolling down her face, she said, "Yea, Yvonne, I heard you." It tore me apart. To this day, when thinking about that day, tears come down my face. She passed away a couple of days later, on September 12, 1994. I love and truly miss my mother so much. She now has peace and is no longer suffering. A *time to be born, and a time to die;* (Eccles.3:2a KJV).

Chapter Four

Dad/My Father

Strong hard working man

My dad was a tall, handsome man from Antiqua. Antiqua is one of the two major islands that make up the Caribbean nation of Antigua and Barbuda in the West Indies. He moved here to the United States at 17 years old and never returned. I remember he told me that he had a brother who lived in New York and was a manager for the county and a brother who played cricket. His mother was black, and his father was white therefore, his complexion was very light. The skin color on his face had gotten dark through the years of working in the sun.

He'd been a boxer before coming to the United States. My family told stories of how strong he was.

One night my mother had driven my dad's car to work and did not have her driver's license. The cops pulled her over, bringing her to my grandmother's house, where they lived. They wanted to talk with my dad, but he was sleeping and did not want anyone to awaken him.

So, the two police officers tried to use force on him, and they may have regretted it. I was told he was about to throw a bicycle on top of one police officer when my grandmother stopped him. They arrested him, and after being released from jail, he lifted his car and turned it around from wherever he had it parked. And, for this reason, I'd say he was strong.

As long as I've known him, he was never a street man. I would describe him as a man that was somewhat particular. A very hard-working man that picked oranges and grapefruits in the fields. During the winter, he would go up north and pick apples and pears. It would be so exciting when he would return home from being upstate New York picking fruit. He would bring back sacks of red and green apples, sometimes pears. The fruit would always be tasty. People would say he was one of the fastest fruit pickers in the field. He made decent wages in his line of work. This is how he made a living and provided for his family.

When he married my mother, she had four sons; therefore, you would not think he had a problem with someone with kids, but my brothers used to say that when eating at the table, he would roll his eyes at them. Maybe he thought they were eating too much. One of my brothers said he took them out into the orange field several times, and he would work them hard.

Early Memories with my Dad

I remember being at the beach as a little girl, and my dad was supposed to be teaching me how to swim. He was pushing my head down, and I was kicking, and I was trying to get up. It felt like I was going to drown. It was a frightening experience. You do not teach someone how to swim by pushing their head down. You hold them up in your arms as a child. This memory has never gone away.

One morning, my dad got so angry with me. He was in the bathroom shaving; I remember he was rolling his eyes at me because of something I had said. He got so angry that he chased me in his undershorts to our next-door neighbor's house. Their back door was unlocked, and I was afraid and just ran into their house. He was running fast behind me; when he got to their door, he swung it open before realizing what he was doing. What was frightening was what would have happened if he had caught me. That was a very intense and scary moment because he was enraged.

My father was furious

One evening my dad, mom, sister, and I after we left my mom's restaurant heading home, we stopped at the store where my aunt would work during the day. There was an elderly couple who owned the store and we were well acquainted with them.

So, the wife of the owner would have this sweat rag she would use to wipe the sweat off her neck and face; when attending to the ribs they sold. She would keep the rag around her neck. This one evening, my dad was teasing her, and she took that dirty sweat rag and hit him across his face with it.

My dad got so angry that he left the store, walked home, and left us in the car. My mother had no driver's license but had to drive the car home. My dad was furious at that woman for hitting him with that nasty rag in his face. She was only teasing him, but he did not like it. He did not find it to be funny at all.

After the divorce

After he and my mother divorced in November 1972, he remarried in June 1973. He married a lady who lived in a subdivision close to where we lived. They all attended the same church, therefore I'm assuming this is where their relationship started.

There were signs

In the years following, my dad was not much in our life. I asked my dad to give me away at our wedding in 1979, and he did, and I appreciated it. Occasionally, I would call and chat with him. My dad never had a relationship with my son or my sister's children. He was more involved with his family, picking their grandkids up from school and being a grandfather. My father wasn't interested in getting to know any of his blood grandchildren and great-grandchildren.

I'd contacted my father once and asked him to walk this bridge with me to talk about some things I was going through, and he agreed to walk with me. I enjoyed the quality time walking and talking with him. It meant so much to me.

When my daughter was married in 2008, I invited him and his wife to the wedding. His wife told me he might not come because he could not buy them a wedding gift. My comment to her was that it was not about a wedding gift. I just wanted him to be there. She did say it was other reasons as well. I do not know what those other reasons were. Maybe they knew something I did not know, maybe, it was a sign of something deeper. But, they attended, and I appreciated it. It made me happy.

When my son passed away; I asked my father, because he had a truck, if he could take me to purchase this bedroom set for my granddaughter. My granddaughter was coming back to live with us, and I did not want to bring the bedroom set from the house where my son was killed. My dad agreed to take me. After we got there, I found something in addition that I wanted to buy and was short a few dollars because I'd taken only enough to pay for the bedroom set.

So, I asked my dad if he would lend it to me until I returned home. After returning home, my father accepted the money he loaned me after giving it back to him and also I gave him money for gas. Prior to him loaning me that money, he's never had to do anything for me or my son, but he took the money. My son, which was his grandson, had just been killed. I did not feel like he should have taken that money from me, especially after never having to do anything for my son and I'm your daughter. That was another sign. I thank God for other than that time, I never needed him for anything.

Losing his eyesight

When I visited his home several times, his wife treated me pleasantly, although we had never been invited to any family gatherings or anything their family had. My dad started losing his eyesight and could not get around on his own. There were times when his wife would want me to pick him up and bring him to our home to spend time with him. I recall driving him and his wife to an appointment he had and I was elated to do that for them.

Rehabilitation center

So after his eyesight got worse, they put him in a rehabilitation center. He thought it was short-term, but he never returned home. After losing his eyesight, I am sure it was tough for him to be in an unfamiliar place. He'd been a deacon in the church for years and had faith, but that was difficult to adjust to. He would share his feelings about the situation. I'd go spend time with him and take him snacks because he would always say he was hungry.

While there, sometimes I'd shave him if he needed it and would also feed him. Sometimes I would take him outside in his wheelchair and sit with him under a tree. We would talk about many things, and he would not want me to leave. He would beg me to stay longer. I felt so sorry for him. He had been such a hard worker all his life; he did not deserve that. I know losing his eyesight had to be difficult for him.

While in the rehab center, his body declined. They were not doing much to rehabilitate him at all. He started not being able to do anything for himself, like standing and walking alone. It was very emotional to see him go through such a drastic change in his life.

He loved his wife and family and would always brag about his oldest stepdaughter and his stepson. They were his favorites. I'd tell him that I did not come here to talk about your stepchildren. I didn't mind, but it was too much. They'd be the only two he would talk about because of their careers. He'd talk and brag about them all the time. He was proud of them for how well he thought they were doing in life. He seemed to measure his feelings about someone based on their status in life, which was sad. The other two daughters were achieving as well.

I'd continue to visit him because he was my father, so I thought, and it was the thing to do. I would often tell people; my sister and I were the only blood family my father had around. I loved him and was so proud of him for being my dad, even if he did nothing for me. This is how much a father means to his daughters.

His passing

On November 20, 2016, my father passed away. He lived to be 89 years old. When he died, his family contacted my sister and informed her of his death. No one cared to notify me of his passing; I assumed they figured my sister would let me know.

When they had his funeral, I wasn't there. I did my part; being there for him when he was alive, therefore, there are no regrets. He knew I loved him. He was shown through my actions how much I loved him.

A time to keep silence and a time to speak;
(Eccles. 3:7 KJV).

My sister told me she tried to introduce her two sons, his grandsons to his wife at his funeral, but she stopped her by telling her it wasn't the time for that. It's all meaningless now, he's gone to a better place to be with the Lord.

Remember: To every thing, there is a season,
(Eccles. 3:1 KJV).

Chapter Five

My Stepfather

My stepfather, the man my mother married in 1972 when she and my dad divorced, was from Ft. Myers, Florida. I believe he met my mother at her restaurant. I supposed he came in and charmed her. He'd been married to a woman in Ft. Myers before marrying my mother, or maybe they lived together. This woman had adult children, but my stepfather wasn't their father. He'd been close to them and claimed them as his own. Also, he and this woman adopted a daughter together. So, he remained in her life while married to my mom and treated her like she was his natural daughter. Therefore, he would always make frequent trips to Ft. Myers. He'd also visit this younger sister who lived in Naples, Florida.

Marriage started out fantastic

Things started out great with their marriage, as most unions do. It appeared he would be a good husband to my mother. He owned his own business, did stucco, and made decent money. Stucco is the texture applied to the outside of a house or building. Therefore, he did his job helping to provide for our family. My mother would buy pretty much whatever she needed. Of course, she worked as well. I called it blessed to have a lovely home decorated to the fullest, able to buy and dress as she desired, and to drive nice cars. My stepfather would exchange cars often and allow me to drive the cars he owned. He even helped my second-oldest brother purchase a Cadillac while in college. So, it seemed she lived a good life for a season.

While attending junior college, my stepfather applied for me as his stepdaughter to receive social security benefits through him. I received a check, and it meant so much to me. I also appreciated it when he shared his insight on different things that would benefit me. When my brother two years older joined the Air Force, he began having reservations about being away from home and started thinking about how he could get out. Our stepfather encouraged him to remain in the service. I am sure my brother respected that wisdom as the years passed, and he retired from the military.

Deception

My mother was a loyal, caring, and faithful wife to her husband. She always tried to please him. I remember seeing her fix his plate of food and she would prepare them like she would at her restaurant. She'd put her love into it, as well as other wifely duties, I'd watch her carry out. That's the type of woman she was, and she taught me to do the same for my husband, even though she and I would butt heads about it.

Later on in the marriage, we started hearing about his womanizing. We heard about several affairs he had with different women throughout their marriage. There were rumors about his relationship with this young girl who lived about a block away from us. She lived a couple of houses down from the neighborhood store where we would go to buy snacks. Teenagers would go there because they had a jukebox in the store, and they loved gathering, meeting friends, dancing, and having fun there.

We were not sure how my stepfather became acquainted with this young lady at his age. We weren't certain whether they met in the store or in passing by her house. He had a habit of sitting under a tree playing the game of checkers with other older men who would flirt with younger women and girls passing. He would prey on them because he had money and nice cars. But my stepfather took it to another level. We started hearing about the young woman driving my mother's Cadillac around town. People were talking about the affair. My mother did not get the chance to learn much about this man's character before she married him because he moved here from out of town. We can think we know someone and then find out we do not know that person at all. A person can really be deceptive. He indeed deceived her, but everything has its time.

Move to Tampa, Florida

My mother could not take it anymore with the disrespect he showed around town. She tried to allow him the opportunity to change and end the affair. Then, it must have been around 1982 when my mother decided to move to Tampa, Florida. At the time, my mother agreed with my sister for her to move into their home and take over the mortgage payments. For whatever reason, my sister never moved into the house. Therefore, the mortgage was not paid because of my mother's inability to care for both places. Even though they moved to Tampa, my stepfather continued to make trips back and forth to Palmetto, continuing his affair with the young lady.

Birth of child

The young lady gave birth to a daughter from my stepfather in June 1983, and based on my calculations, she was 24 years old, and he was the age of 61. So, he and my mother separated for a while and divorced in 1985. However, he and my mother continued to communicate with one another. But he and the young lady moved into an apartment and started living together in Palmetto for some time. In 1994, they purchased a home together in Bradenton. In 1995, my stepfather fathered a son with her.

It was a rumor that my stepfather was giving money to the young lady to make the mortgage payments on their home; however, she saved the money to leave him instead of making the payments. So, their home foreclosed in 1999, and things started going downhill for him. He ended up at some point moving to an apartment for seniors and turning his life around, joining a church, and becoming a deacon, even though I am not sure of the correct order of this change that took place in his life.

He treated me like his daughter

Regardless of how things worked out with him and my mother, he treated me with respect. He acted more like a father to me than my dad. My sister did not like being around him. She told me she got married to get out of the house. Once, when my mother went to the hospital for surgery, my second oldest brother came to live with us because my sister did not want us to be alone with him. He had shown my sister a different side.

One day, my stepfather was bragging and told me and my husband that he began a relationship with the young girl when she was a teenager. I question why he cared to share that information with us because today, having an affair at his age with someone that young would not be taken lightly. He also told me the young lady's mother knew about him having an affair with her during her teenage years.

My mother just made a terrible choice in her selection of him. As women, we need to think more carefully about the men we choose and bring into our homes. Especially when we have children. My father/dad was an angel in comparison to my stepfather as it relates to certain behaviors. The grass is not always greener on the other side.

In a relationship, if we do not take the time to find out who someone is as an individual, we will indeed run into problems if we are chasing love, money, and what we think is security. My stepfather brought my mother down. *A time to love, and a time to hate;* (Eccles. 3:8a KJV). She never hated him. I am sure she hated his actions. I know she forgave him, even though he had taken her on an emotional roller coaster and was responsible for her losing everything.

After he fell ill and started living in a convalescent home, I visited him, and when he needed some dental work done I took care of it because of his kindness to me. He passed away on May 23, 2007. My husband and I attended his funeral. *A time to mourn,* (Eccles. 3:4b KJV).

Forgave her

Years later, when working at one of my many jobs, this lady came into the office to enquire about buying a house. So, when she walked through the door, we were familiar. I treated her like any other person who walked through the door. Then, after providing her with the information she needed, she hugged me and cried. She felt guilty for my treating her the way God would have me to, with love and respect, after knowing she destroyed my mother's marriage and caused her so much pain. The young lady was young and selfish, but I had to forgive her. We all make mistakes, and if she has asked for forgiveness, God has forgiven her. I am sure she is reaping what she has sowed because we all will. *Be not deceived; God is not mocked: for whatsoever a man soweth, that shall he also reap,* (Gal. 6:7 KJV).

A time to keep silence, and a time to speak;
(Eccles. 3:7 KJV).

Chapter Six

My Grandmother

My grandmother, my mother's mother, gave birth to two children: my mother and uncle. We never met my mother's father, and my mother never talked about him. My grandmother never talked about my mother's father either, but she had supposedly been married to him. She had also been married to my uncle's father, and my uncle was named after him. My grandmother and my uncle's father purchased a home together. I was told my grandmother would always pray to God for her husband to turn his life around.

A widow

My mom, I was told, wanted my grandmother to buy her something when she was a little girl, and when my grandmother told her husband, my mother's stepfather, he supposedly commented, "Over my dead body." Later that night, as was told to me, he went out and someone stabbed him to death. *Death and life are in the power of the tongue:* (Proverbs 18:21 KJV). My grandmother never remarried. I only knew her as a widow.

We would tease her constantly, telling her she needed a husband. This older gentleman who lived down the street in his charming home was blind. His wife must have passed away. He walked with his cane as he would pass my grandmother's house. You can tell he was a well-to-do man. He would always be dressed nicely. Joking with my grandmother, I'd tell her he should be her husband. They appeared to be around the same age. She would just smile because she was not interested in having a companion.

My great-grandfather, my grandmother's father, was a stern man. I remember him watching over us when we were younger. So, he lived around the corner from my grandmother and down the street from my aunt. He'd cook lima beans, rice,

and cornbread all the time. We all called him
Grandpapa. I loved my grandpapa, even though he
was mean. My great-grandmother was an Indian
woman, and looking at her picture, it seems like she
could have been a mean strict woman. But I never
had a chance to meet her.

Everyone has a past before God changes them
from sinners to saints. I heard stories about my
grandmother later in life; according to them, she did
not play; she would hurt someone if they bothered
her or her family. My only experience of her
growing up was… she loved the Lord and lived to
serve Him.

Could not read or write

My grandmother could not read or write but
could read the Bible. She didn't only talk about the
word of God; she lived it. She helped start up the
church we attended years ago and would have bible
lessons at her house to teach kids in the
neighborhood during the summer. She would have
me go to church members' houses to pick up their
tithes.

As a child, I experienced being told; God
would strike me down when I asked specific
questions about God and certain things in the Bible.

My grandmother would say to me; you do not question God. I would ask her, "Well, doesn't God want me to know?" I would then tell her; that I do not want to serve a God that will strike me down for trying to understand. I would ask, "Grandma, why would a loving God strike me down for asking questions about him?" She did not understand. It was her way of putting the fear of God in us.

Around twelve years old, she would have me come to her house and write letters to different family members living out of town. She would always have me start the letter's salutation with: "Dear so and so, I am saved today and have a sound mind to live right." It was how she would always have me begin her letters. Then, when I'd leave her house and say to her, "See you later, grandma," or "See you tomorrow, grandma." She'd say, "If it's God's will, darling."

She was a strict woman

She was a strict woman. I remember calling her one day when I was upset with my mother. I wanted my grandmother to hear my side and her response was, "She is your mother, and you do not argue with her." That was it. It was a conversation I would not be having with her. We were taught to respect our parents and elders.

As a teenager, she asked me to go to the store for her one day. Once I'd gotten to her house and she saw the short shorts I was wearing, she looked at me and said, "That's ok, darling." She did not want me to go to the store, representing her wearing those shorts. To this day, I'm conscious about what I wear.

It was this song that this famous blind singer wrote, and I was unaware when I was a little girl that it was a rhythm and blues song. So, my grandmother heard me singing it one day. She called me into the house and gave me a good whipping with what they called a switch. I didn't know at the time why I was getting a whipping. It was because it was a non-Christian song, and I was not supposed to sing it. Not around her anyway.

Her trust was in God

I never heard my grandmother complain about anything. Her trust was in God Almighty. She was a praying woman, and God took care of her. She would have me come over and make out her monthly bills. Her home was paid off, and she was only receiving social security and a few dollars in food stamps, but she lived well on that little income she had coming in monthly. She appeared to have everything she needed.

Chapter Six: My Grandmother

I'd recall my grandmother being very particular about certain things. She would keep her silverware, cup, glass, and plate separate from the rest. She did not want anyone else using the utensils she would use to eat or drink. She kept her house very clean. She would have me come over on weekends to dust her furniture and give me a few dollars.

Before she passed away, she said, "You will always be blessed." She also told me she did not want to leave this earth, not knowing that I had not given my life to Christ. She loved serving the Lord. She taught me things like; never to accept money from a man if you are not married because he would think he owned me. And not to become common with a man if you are not married. Her meaning was… for me not to live with someone before getting married. She taught me many things, but those stuck with me.

Even though my grandmother lived in her home around the corner, she hardly ever visited our house. The bus would let her out at the end of our street, and she would walk past our home. I never knew why she would not visit. She attended our reception at our house when my husband and I were married, but she rarely stopped at our home. My grandaunt, her sister, would visit us, and she resided across the street from my grandmother. She and her sister were very close. Before her sister, my grandaunt passed away, my grandmother had been told by God that He was going to take her sister. My grandmother begged God to take her first and not her sister. He took her sister. I was told my grandmother did not care to live anymore when her sister, my grandaunt passed away.

A praying woman

My grandmother was one of my mentors, she meant so much to me, and I admired her. Seeing this woman who could not read or write but could read the Bible was amazing. She knew the Bible and could teach it. She loved God and everything the Bible stood for. She was a praying woman and believed in the power of speaking in tongues. She had the gift, and it was not for a show because she would do it in the privacy of her bedroom with her door closed.

She later developed sugar. Today, you do not hear that term much; it is type II diabetes. She managed her diabetes very well. She would watch what she ate, but as she got older, it must have become harder for her to manage. I remember seeing her when she would get off the bus down the street from our home and walk by the house, she would have a little difficulty walking. It may have been due to foot pain related to diabetic neuropathy.

Due to her diabetes, she ended up having both legs amputated. As her sickness progressed, my third oldest brother, living with her, took care of her like a child; he administered her insulin shots three times a day. He would give her baths, clean, cook, and be there for whatever she needed. He was right by her side. She passed away on December 21, 1988. God blessed her to live to be 83 years old. *A time to mourn,* (Eccles. 3:4b KJV). A great woman of God.

Chapter Seven

Grandaunt

The matriarch of the family

My grandaunt was a humble, beautiful, kind God-fearing woman. She and my granduncle never had any children. Supposedly, she was 13 years old when she got married. Whereas, my granduncle was 39 years old at the time and lived to be 118 years old.

She always lived very well and never had to worry much about anything. For the majority of her life, she did not have to work. But, she would assist at this neighborhood store part-time, which was within walking distance of their home, because she and the owner were friends. She was always there for the family whenever we needed her support of any kind. I considered her the matriarch of the family.

She and her husband owned a home across the street from her sister, my grandmother. They had a large shed on their property with all kinds of tools and lawn equipment for my granduncle's lawn maintenance business. And, they owned a chicken coup where they raised chickens and produced eggs. My granduncle worked hard for many years, and they had accumulated a lot.

A faithful church member

She was a faithful church member who significantly contributed to church fundraisings. Back then, your name would be displayed on the side of the church pew if you made a significant enough contribution to pay for one.

My grandaunt and grandmother's sister lived in another city with her husband and they owned their home. She was the youngest and never had any children either. She had been close to her sisters before they passed away. She departed on June 16, 1999. Furthermore, they had three brothers, one of whom died years ago after being killed inside his barbershop. He had three children, and based on my knowledge they were two daughters and one son.

Allegedly, he has a daughter that lived in the town where I grew up. She has been deceased for many years and some of her family members do not want to accept that my granduncle was her father.

My granduncle's daughter

My granduncle's daughter lives in Miami, Florida. She was close to my mother, being her first cousin and my grandaunt and grandmother's niece. After I finished high school, this cousin wanted me to live with her and her family and attend Miami Dade College. Being a mother's girl, I stayed there for about two weeks and was ready to go home. I can't imagine the possibilities of how my life may have been if I had remained in Miami with her, but God had other plans for me.

Amazingly, this is just a tiny portion of this cousin's achievements, because she has done so much in her life. I would have to write another book covering all her accomplishments and state and community involvement through the years. She has received an Honorary Doctorate from FAMU College, a Bachelor's Degree from Fayetteville University, and a Master's of Education Degree from the University of Miami. She retired as a Miami-Dade Public Schools Administrator and was an advocate for human rights and equality in Florida. As well as was president of the Florida NAACP and sat on the civil rights organization's national board. She gave birth to three children who also have Bachelor's and Master's degrees, and one is seeking her doctorate. They are doing great things.

For years, one of my granduncles was a barber on Central Avenue in Sarasota, Florida, and he passed away in 1983. He would come to visit his sisters every Sunday when he was able to get around. He would also stop by my mother's home, always bringing a pocket full of change to give quarters to the kids. He had a son who lived in Miami with his family. He, his wife, and one of their sons have passed away, but he still has children living in Florida and other places.

My grandaunt had another brother who had a different father from their mother and lived in Havana, Florida, and he passed away around 1986. Many family members live in Havana on their brother's side, but I have never had the opportunity to meet them.

A heart attack

When my second oldest brother got his high school sweetheart pregnant in her first year in college, her aunt, who raised her, did not want her to have a child. Therefore, my grandaunt agreed to care for their baby while the mother continued college. In the meantime, my grandaunt had gotten very attached to him because she had never had kids. Then, four years later, his mother and father contacted my grandaunt and told her they were coming to get their son because she had completed her schooling. My grandaunt was hurt after realizing that she would have to give him up. She went to her sister's house, my grandmother, and told her she's been praying to God and she has to let him go.

Then she went home and slept, but never woke up. She had never been sick, not even a headache. She had a heart attack. It was too much for her, she had gotten so attached to him, and it was devastating to her having to give him up. This was when God showed my grandmother, he was going to take her sister and she prayed for God to take her first. My grandaunt was ready to go. My nephew was lying beside her when she passed away in her bed on January 9, 1975. She was 65, and my nephew was four years old at the time. However, he is the poet with the deep voice mentioned earlier, whose alter ego name is "Coco Brown." So, his parents returned to Palmetto and moved into my aunt's house for a short while until moving to

Bradenton, then Gainesville, Florida. Then, my mother took my granduncle to live with us until he died.

Before my aunt passed, she would travel to Havana, Florida, and my brother, who is two years older, would travel with her to see her relatives on my great-grandmother's side. My brother, with whom my aunt kept their son, has also traveled to Havana with her. So, we have all these relatives on my grandaunt and grandmother's side living in Havana. One of them was a college professor. Surprisingly, my grandaunt supposedly had land and money that was passed down to her. She died allegedly having plenty of money in her house and bank account. It has been somewhat of a mystery what happened to it.

To every thing there is a season, and a time for every purpose under the heaven: (Eccles. 3:1 KJV).

Chapter Eight

Uncle, My Mother's Brother

Outstanding football player

My uncle, my mother's brother, was born to my grandmother when she was 38. He was a nicely built, handsome guy. There were rumors that he was my mother's child, but it isn't true. Before going into the military, he had been an outstanding football player at Lincoln High School in Palmetto and could have gone to try out to play professionally.

Chapter Eight: Uncle, My Mother's Brother

He married a church member before being drafted into the army. He and his wife had two sons together. While in the army, his wife left him and moved to New York, and she never returned. I was told she left because she did not like her husband sending his money home to his mother. So, this caused him to become heartbroken and, therefore, he reenlisted in the military.

"My son is not dead"

I never had a chance to meet my cousins. They never came back to Florida. After his second time in the army during the Vietnam War, my uncle witnessed many casualties and was supposedly killed. According to my third oldest brother, a representative from the military came to my grandmother's house to inform her that her son had been killed and to provide her with a flag. A flag symbolizes the honor earned and the sacrifice made in battle while serving America. My grandmother told them, "Take that flag and leave, my son is not dead. He is alive, and God is not going to take my son and not tell me."

According to my brother, my grandmother went back into her room and started speaking in tongues, talking to God. I can't recall how long it was after they came and gave her that terrifying news concerning her son; he walked through the door and arrived back home safe from the military. Consequently, when he returned from fighting the second time, he was in shell shock. Today, it is called PTSD (Post-Traumatic Stress Disorder).

Disturbed

My uncle told me his friend suffered a casualty after a bomb hit him. He picked up his deceased friend and carried his body back to the barracks. For his heroic actions, he received a medal. They considered my uncle a hero. When he returned home, all he had witnessed in the military disturbed him.

When he would ride in the car with us, and an airplane would fly over, he would duck down in the car and shield his head. The Vietnam War destroyed him; he was never the same, so you did not want to make him mad. So, my husband and I would sometimes take him back and forth to Bay Pines Veterans Hospital in St. Petersburg, Fl. for medical treatments.

He began drinking heavily after he returned home. My grandmother started hiding her mouthwash. When he could not buy alcohol, I was told he would drink the mouthwash because of the alcohol content. Family members were afraid of him. Mentally, he was dealing with a lot and needed help. It affected his relationships with women and he would sometimes get physical with them. The police were called to the house one day. When they came inside the house, my uncle was sitting in his rocking chair, shaking his feet, and would not move. The police eventually left and would not do anything.

My brother, which lived with my grandmother and uncle, eventually moved out of the house for a while because he feared him. Our grandmother had to be taken to our mother's house one day because my uncle was having a bad day and threatened her. She was afraid her son would hurt her. Everyone knew not to aggravate him.

I once had an encounter with my uncle that involved him chasing me around my grandmother's house. It wasn't much chasing because my uncle could run fast. I was a runner but would have never been able to outrun him. He caught me and used this technique, where he took both of his hands and grabbed my collarbone, and squeezed it. All I could do was stand on my tippy toes and cry because I could not do anything. It was so painful until he let me go. I never did anything to upset him again. I can't recall what I did that time to anger him.

He was a hard worker and would always get a job where they built boats. He was a nice, soft-spoken man when he wasn't angry. He never had a problem meeting a nice woman, but the relationship would not last long because of his anger issues. He had two other sons out of wedlock. One lived with his mother, my grandmother for a short while before returning to Rochester, New York, where his mother lived. He has since passed away. His other son lives here in Florida.

For some reason, he and my mother did not get along very well, and I never knew why. Before my uncle passed away, he told my brother he was dying and that our mother, his sister, would be next.

Early death

Unfortunately, he didn't get to live a more meaningful life before passing away. He never got the opportunity to heal or mend. His broken heart from his wife leaving him with his two children and never seeing them again, along with his experiences in the military, took their toll on him, and he could never get over it.

Chapter Eight: Uncle, My Mother's Brother

He died young, and so have many others. He passed away on September 20, 1991, from diabetes complications, three years before his sister, my mother. They both passed away from diabetes complications and so did their mother. Before he passed away, he was dealing with much anger and possibly resentment. As far as I know, he did not make peace with his maker. I pray God knew his heart and what he was dealing with. He was 48 years old. He is no longer suffering. I pray that God will continue to bless his soul because He knows all about his adversities. *A time of war, and a time of peace* (Eccles. 3:8b KJV). I also pray he is at peace with the Lord. *He hath made every thing beautiful in his time.* (Eccles. 3:11 KJV)

Chapter Nine

Adulthood

I would like to meet you

In 1979, I began working my first real job for
the city and a part-time job in the evenings at the
Bradenton Harold. At The Harold, I worked as a
telephone solicitor, making calls to households,
expecting a sale by getting them to sign up for home
delivery of the newspaper. On this one evening call,
a young man was on the other end of the line. After
introducing myself, I followed my script; do you
have the Bradenton Harold delivered to your home?
His reply was, "No." My next question was, would
you like the paper delivered to your home? His
answer was "Yes." Then I collected the additional
information needed to distribute the newspaper to
his home. The sale had been achieved. Afterward,

the personal questions started. What's your name?
Blah, blah, blah.

At some point, I ended up telling my sister
about the conversation I had with the guy. So, one
day, my sister said, "You know that guy you told
me about? He called for you." Then one day, I
decided to return the call to him. I learned my sister
had lied. He had never called for me. But, during
our conversation, he said, "I would like to meet
you." So, we talked a little, and he shared that he
was home from attending Delta State University
College in Cleveland, Mississippi, for the summer.
For some reason, my interest in meeting him was
just not there. I was content and did not want to be
in a committed relationship.

That was the beginning

Eventually, we agreed to meet and we set a day
and time to connect. On that day; my friend, who
was my next-door neighbor, agreed to drive me to
where he lived in the projects. He was living with
his mother while home from college. We arranged
to drive her car so that I would be on the passenger
side. If he did not look like someone I would be
interested in dating, we would continue to ride by
and not stop. So, when we arrived at the apartment,
three people were standing outside on the porch. It

was two guys and a girl. One was a tall, handsome guy who was pleasing to the eye. The other two were his brother and his sister. Consequently, his reason for having his brother and sister out there was; that he would pretend to be his brother if I did not meet his expectations. We both found one another appealing. That was the beginning.

The next night, as we were talking on the telephone, he mentioned he was hungry, which was kind of late. I offered to pick him up and take him to get something to eat because he did not have a car. Since then, he continue to mention how my kindness that night won him over.

As we continued to communicate, he shared that he and his mother moved to Ft. Myers, Florida, from Bradenton in the ninth grade. And after he graduated, his mother moved back to Bradenton. He said he attended Dunbar High School the first year, then; he attended Riverdale High School during his remaining high school years, where he graduated. But, before he graduated high school at Riverdale, he became known for his basketball abilities and was awarded a basketball scholarship to attend Edison Community College. So, he completed two years at Edison and, thereupon, received another scholarship to attend Delta State University in

Mississippi. While at Delta State, he returned home to help his mother while she was ill. Therefore, he never returned back to complete his education after we started dating.

He accepted my child

When my grandmother met and approved of him, it was determined that he would be the right one. What was most important to me was that he accepted my child. My son adored him. He was what I called a gentleman. After he proposed to me and I accepted it, I asked my father if he would give me away at our wedding, and he agreed. We were married on November 17, 1979. My father was there to give me away. My son was our ring bearer; he was seven, almost eight years old at the time. God is good!

So, we had a lovely wedding. My neighbor next door, a school teacher, was our wedding planner. Our wedding was at the church our family attended. We had four bridesmaids; my sister-in-law, my best friend, and two other friends. My sister was my maid of honor, and my niece, her daughter, was the flower girl. Since I had learned how to sew, I made my wedding dress, the flower girl's, and the maid of honor's dresses. Two of my friends and my sister-in-law made their dresses. I cannot recall if it was my neighbor's friend or me that made my other friend's dress. Knowing how to sew saved us a lot.

My husband's best man was my classmate. He would be so mean to me in school. I would doze off in the classroom in middle school, and he would harass me, throwing spitballs at me. He was a bully; I did not care for him in school. He became pastor in his father's church either before his father passed away or after and is now a different man. He is now my friend as well as my husband's. The groomsmen were my brother, my best friend's boyfriend, a classmate, and a friend.

The reception was held at my mother's house, where she used her skills and beautifully prepared all except the cake. Everything was well prepared. My mother did a fantastic job. Our mayor of the city attended. And many of my close friends were in attendance as well. Marriage was far from my mind, and God brought me a husband when I wasn't even looking for one. Everything has its time. It was God's plan for my life.

Once we joined in marriage, it came with in-laws. I gained a mother-in-law, a father-in-law, a stepmother-in-law, four sisters-in-laws, and one brother-in-law. He has since lost his brother and lost one of his twin sisters to cancer. My husband acquired a mother-in-law and step-father-in-law, with whom we have lost both, one sister-in-law, and four brothers-in-law. I always felt that my in-laws thought I hindered my husband from completing his college education and from having the opportunity to try out for basketball by not remaining in college. However, I had nothing to do with his decision not to return to school. I had been encouraging him to go back.

Established credit

Driving my red and white Mustang with a tag on the front that read, "Single and Loves it." Thanks to the city clerk at the time. With my lack of credit, the city clerk thought enough of me to call the bank president to approve a loan for my ford mustang. So, I will never forget what that city clerk did for me. He helped me obtain credit. Although I had thanked him already; many years later; sitting and thinking about how good God had been to me, it was laid on my heart to send him a thank you card and thank him again.

What he did for me was appreciated. He helped me get my first car loan when I had no credit. I had no one willing to co-sign for me, or they were not in a position to. I am genuinely grateful for that act of kindness to this day. Thank you, God! "Everything

Has Its Time." The city clerk's response was, "You did it yourself by making your payments," and he was right. He opened the door and helped me establish credit, but I honored and maintained it. Again, my prayer is, thank you, God, for everything.

Move to St. Petersburg

So, after we were married, I resigned from the city job after my oldest brother, who worked for Kenny Shoe store, helped my husband get a salesman job with Kenny Shoe Store at Tyrone Square Mall in St. Petersburg, Fl. We moved to St. Petersburg into an apartment at a large apartment complex not far from the Skyway Bridge. I applied for a bank's proof operator position and was hired.

One day, my husband and I were at home, and there was a knocking at the door. When I answered, a young lady was standing there; she asked for my husband. He went out and spoke with her. They talked outside for a few minutes. My thought at the time was that I must not have supposed to have been home.

My husband explained that she was a customer who had visited the store where he worked. He said that he and an employee were talking about where they were from and where they lived the day she was there. Then, the customer joined the conversation and supposedly said to my husband, "Oh, you live in Bellefonte Apartments." He said he never told her where he lived in the complex. But, on that day, she somehow found her way to the apartment whether he told her or not. I never knew what to think of that. She was a very bold woman to come and knock at our door. Even to remain there after I opened it. He said he got her straight and told her not to return to the apartment again because he was married. I was calm about the situation and did not say anything to her. As a shoe salesman, my husband would interact with women daily. He was a friendly, tall attractive man and dressed for the job. He was a great salesman when he worked for the shoe store. He has a charming personality, and you must have a friendly disposition if you want to make those sales, and he was good at it.

An embarrassing moment

He experienced this embarrassing moment when he went to Allstate Insurance in St. Pete to apply for a position. While there, he asked someone where the restroom was, and he was instructed to go through the two doors, keep straight through to the next set of doors, and turn left. He followed the instructions, and he said; when he opened the two doors, it was a room full of females typing, and they all stopped at once, looking at him. He said he was so embarrassed and would not forget that moment. And, he had to come back through those same doors.

Move to Ocala, Florida, and back

My husband had accepted a promotion with Kenny Shoe Store that would have moved us to Ocala, Fl. He had gone to Ocala for about a month to help set up the new store at their new Paddock Mall that opened in 1980. While there that month, he found an apartment not far from the mall for us to move into. He returned to St. Petersburg on a Friday, and we loaded up a rental truck with all our belongings to move us both there.

We needed to get back to Ocala before 5:00 pm on Friday to have the lights turned on in the apartment. We were on the road; we were not going to make it on time; my husband called his co-manager and asked him; if he could do him a favor by putting up a deposit until we got there to have our lights turned on in the apartment. We would have been without lights in the apartment over the weekend if we did not get them turned on that day.

The co-manager responded, "We didn't even know where you were." My husband explained that it was his day off, and he didn't need to tell him where he was going. The conversation did not go very well; however, I told my husband this was not a good sign, so let's go back home. We stayed overnight in a hotel, got up the following morning, and drove back to my mother's house in Palmetto. We figured it was not God's plan for our life. Everything has its time.

On Monday morning, I called the City and informed them of what happened, and was told to come to work the next day. I had been gone from the City for about a year, and they hired me back. I'd advised my husband to go to Tropicana and apply for a job. Tropicana had him come back every day for two weeks before he could get an interview. So, he finally got interviewed, and in the conversation, they told my husband that he had a black mark on his application. Consequently, it was an indication not to rehire; because he had been employed there and worked one night on the night shift and did not return. Therefore, Personnel had him return many times to determine how badly he wanted the job. So, he was hired as a laboratory technician trainee in September 1980.

Purchased our first home

My husband had been employed with Tropicana for a few weeks when my mother informed us about a man who had a foreclosed home on 20th Ave E. in Bradenton that he was trying to sell. Buying a home was the last thing on our minds. We had not given purchasing a home a thought. So, we talked with the gentleman, went to look at the house, and became very fascinated with the possibility of becoming a homeowner. Then, we began inquiring about the steps we needed to take. We learned that we would need to be on the job for at least six months or more to qualify for a mortgage. And we would also need a down payment of eighteen hundred dollars, which we did not have at the time.

We were excited as long as we could work those two things out. So we agreed to make monthly payments to the seller until we come up with the earnest money. We also consented to fix up the property during that time. When we started fixing the house, mounds of cut grass were left in the yard, and many snakes were under those mounds. My stepfather helped us rehabilitate the house. He applied stucco on the outside and plastered the inside. The inside was dark with brown paneling throughout, and it lightened the interior when plastered with white.

We would get the Shopping Guide that came out every Wednesday, where we could purchase used items. We bought some nice carpet and had it installed throughout. Everything worked out, and we obtained our first home on April 1, 1981, seven months after my husband started working at Tropicana. God is good all the time.

Feeling of violation

While living at my mother's house, we came home from work one day, and someone had broken into the house. The person stole my husband's shoes, clothing, and jewelry. They even stole his underclothing. When someone comes and takes the things you have worked hard to obtain, you feel violated. There is nothing you can do about it. You do not know who has come into your private space and has taken what belongs to you. You wonder, are they coming back again? You feel unsafe, as though someone is watching you. It was reported, but no one was ever arrested for the break-in, but we had our suspicions.

We thought it might be this guy my stepfather had been talking with and perhaps bragging about what he owned. The guy had spent many of his teenage years in jail for burglary, etc. He and my stepfather had been seen together, sitting and talking at the youth center behind my mother's home. I also wondered if my stepfather was involved. My mother had this large sum of money she had just gotten from a financial transaction, and it was under her mattress and taken. We were able through insurance to recoup some of the losses, but it still does not erase the feeling of violation.

Enjoying life

So, life continued with us living as young adults raising a family in our first home. We enjoyed life with our close friends traveling together, having house parties, going to parties, and having fun. We went on a family trip to Atlanta a couple of times and visited the Martin Luther King Dream Center; it was impressive and educational. We visited the Underground Atlanta and the Lennox Square Mall shopping and sightseeing. It was breathtaking. We enjoyed it.

My husband and I met a couple at this restaurant in Atlanta. We were looking for a place we could get some crabs, and they were familiar with a place where we would be able to buy some. They invited us to follow them there; we purchased the crabs, went to their house, cooked, and ate them together. They were visiting from Maryland and loved crabs like my husband. The mother of one of them ate everything on the crabs, which was amazing to me. They were friendly and pleasant people. It was a pleasure meeting them and spending time with them.

On another trip to Atlanta, we took my husband's niece, his sister's daughter. Getting out of the car to go into Six Flags over Georgia; I won't ever forget, somehow, her finger was slammed into the door. That horrendous scream took some time to leave my memory. I felt terrible for her, but the excitement at Six Flags eventually helped her overcome the pain.

On my husband's side, we traveled to Atlanta and Macon, Georgia, for family reunions. His father was from Sparta, Georgia. Therefore, he has family all over Georgia. Every time we would attend a family reunion, we would not remain throughout the event because the families attending would seem to be social only to the group they were close with.

Outstanding basketball player

My husband does not know many of his family members on his father's side, and it concerned him why his father never took him to Sparta to meet his family. It was also an issue for him that his father never attended any basketball games he played when he was younger. He said his father attended his graduation and had no idea his son was considered an outstanding basketball player at his school.

It wasn't until his name was called to walk up to receive his diploma that the students started chanting his name and gave him a standing ovation. This was when his father realized his son was a basketball star at his high school. It also bothered him that his father did not give him anything for his graduation.

He was the Southwest Florida leading scorer and Player of the Year, All-Southwest Florida first team. Riverdale High School Basketball Team Most Valuable Player and Riverdale High School Most Outstanding Athlete in 1975. He was known as "Chicken."

A conscious decision

It also concerned him when he was younger that his father would pick him and his sister up on Fridays and drop them off where he lived with his girlfriend. He remembers his father would shower and leave the house, and they would not see him again until he returned to take them home. His girlfriend, who my husband described as a very sweet lady, would care for them. He would always tell me that because of how his father treated him, he wanted to be married to the mother of his children so that he could be there for his family. So he made a conscious decision not to have children with different women everywhere. And, as far as he knows, he only has one biological child.

My husband also has a sister his father had from his live-in girlfriend and believes his father was involved in her life. His sister has a brother who played basketball and was an outstanding player. I was told he had a severe knee injury which hindered his playing and set him back. He played in college with players that went on to be professional basketball players. My husband said his father used to attend his games in high school. I told my husband it may have been because he lived in Ft. Myers, and his father, his sister, and her brother lived in Palmetto; therefore, it was easier for him to attend his games. Later his father married a woman, and they had two children, a son and a daughter together. My husband knew his father was spending quality time with the two kids, taking them to and from their sports activities. The son played baseball, and the daughter played softball. Therefore, he had resentment towards him because he was not there for him as a father. It bothered him deeply and still does.

When my husband first met his stepmother, he said he did not get good vibes from her. He would always say, it's something about her even though she appeared to be sweet and kind. In 1994, his father passed away from a sudden heart attack in his bed. His wife had already left to go to work. Supposedly, his father had been up earlier and gone back to bed. So, when one of the kids went into the bedroom to awaken him to take them to school, he was found deceased. However, as they were leaving with his body, the wife left the house to go to a hair salon. We thought it was a little different, but maybe it was her way of grieving. Before he died, she had been using a cane to help her walk, and once he passed away, she was no longer using the cane when we would see her out and about.

My husband tried to reach out to his stepmother after his father died, and she avoided him. He contacted her and even set up a time to meet her at their home, but she would not answer the door. Before his father's death, again, she appeared to be a sweet and kind lady. I happened to run into her children, my husband's siblings, at the mall a few weeks after their dad's death. I asked them how they were doing and then went on to ask them, why they did not want to have anything to do with their brother. And, I think it was his brother that responded, "Because of how he treated our dad." However, as I was talking to them, their mother walked up and told me to leave them alone. She then said to me; they would come around when they were ready. Her behavior towards me was certainly strange. Seemingly, they were unaware of the relationship between their father and brother or were too young to understand.

My husband did not try to contact his stepmother anymore. He had never been disrespectful to her or exchanged any words with her. Again she did not start acting that way until his father passed away. People will show you who they are, and when they do, believe it. Everything has its time.

He has since spoken with his brother, but not his sister. We were told she had moved to Georgia. I have become Facebook friends with many of his family members on his father's side, but many of them are distant relatives.

We enjoyed trips

We took the kids on summer trips to Orlando many times and visited many attractions there. The one where we took our daughter and her friend to St. Augustine, Florida was more educational, and they enjoyed it. They also visited Daytona Beach and had plenty of fun there.

Our family traveled to New Orleans and took my second oldest brother's daughter along when they were teenagers. It was exciting to see all those European-style architectural buildings. We visited some of the tourist attractions. We stayed in the beautiful Bourbon Orleans Hotel and walked along Bourbon Street and other streets, enjoying the music, looking at the strange people, and enjoying all the food. While cruising on the boat along the Mississippi River, we savored dinner with the family and had a wonderful time. It was a memorable trip.

Our chosen land

In June 1999, my husband's best friend, whose wife and I are also friends, told us about this land out east. We went together to check it out and there were a few homes built in the subdivision. Most of the property around was cow pastures and there were no stores anywhere close.

We decided we liked the area and would be interested in building a home one day on the chosen land. First, we called a bank and inquired about a loan to buy the property. We learned there would be no problem getting it financed. Then, we contacted the seller to let him know we were interested in purchasing the acre. After an appraisal, we obtained funding in June 1990.

We had this young pastor and his wife ministering at a church my mother had started attending while living with us. They would come to visit us at our home often. The wife said one day, "You all are going to be in that house much sooner than you think." It was like she was prophesying to me. We were not planning on building anytime soon when we made the purchase.

However, in 21 months, on March 3, 1992, we were approved for a construction loan to build the house. We met with a contractor and determined the design of the home we would like to have constructed and what amenities we would include. The builder provided us with the contract price and breakdown cost of everything. After reviewing it all, we agreed and signed the commitment. We

would receive an addendum to the agreement if any
changes or additions occurred. We were told the
house was to be completed in six months.

We arranged with my sister to move in with her
in her apartment until the house was built because
we had already rented the house we were living in
out to a renter. So, we agreed to pay my sister an
amount towards her rent and buy our groceries.
Well, that agreement lasted a short while. My sister
and I had a significant fallout about something I
was alleged to have said about her to this guy she
had just met. She was so angry, she threw
something at me that could have injured me, but in
time, I forgave her. She and this guy eventually
ended up getting married. The guy turned out to be
abusive, and the marriage did not last long.

We could not be choosey

We moved out immediately and did not have a
place to stay. We had to move into my mother's
one-bedroom apartment for about two weeks.
Finding a place to live was difficult because no one
would let us do a short-term lease on an apartment.
The lease would have to be for twelve months or
more. Therefore, we found this empty duplex that
was in a complete state of disarray. For a short
lease, we convinced the owners to allow us to move

in, in exchange for cleaning up the duplex. They
agreed. But filthy does not describe the apartment's
condition. We needed a place to stay until our house
was completed; therefore, we could not be choosey.

The previous renters were going through a
breakup, we were told, and someone must have
been very depressed. They were throwing
everything in the middle of the living room instead
of in the trash. Over the front door post was a sock
hanging with an egg inside with writing on it; it was
the same way over the bedroom doors. The place
was a complete mess. But we decided to do what
we needed to do, to move into that apartment. When
we finished, it looked like a different place inside.
We were very proud of how everything looked after
we were completed.

The only problem we had was this little black
slimy housemate in the kitchen when I would come
home each day. It would run and hide in the cabinet
where the pots and pans were. Every day I would be
afraid to go into the kitchen because it would
always run and hide. You did not know what day
you would open the cabinet and it would be there.
So, this went on for about a week or so. Determined
to get it out, we finally sneaked up on it and killed

that slimy black lizard. It gives me the creeps thinking about it.

Lien notices in the mail

We would check on the house as it was being built, but not as regularly as we should have. My husband did not feel the need to, but it was needed. The progress should have been moving along better. My neighbor was asking why work was not regularly done on the house. We then started getting all these lien notices in the mail where the builder was not paying the subcontractors for the work they had completed.

Usually, a builder, when building a home, is not paid upfront for building a house. The bank will pay the builder by bank draws/funds from the construction loan you borrowed. The builder may get seven bank draws or less throughout the home-building process until it's completed. The bank is supposed to be responsible for ensuring that the builder has completed certain portions of the house when they provide the builder with the funds. And the customer is supposed to sign off on those draws from the bank to the builder.

And the builder is supposed to make sure he pays his subcontractors. In our case, the builder had not been paying his subcontractors, and when he did not, they placed mechanic's liens on our property. A mechanic's lien is a legal claim against your property. When we called the bank near the end concerning all the lien notices, we learned the remaining funds were the last draw, and the amount was insufficient to pay all the lien holders and the county for impact fees which were necessary. The county imposes a fee on new construction to help with providing public services.

So, we advised the bank to hold the last check from the builder and instructed them to pay the nine subcontractors that had placed liens on the property and to pay the county. The builder begged us to ensure the county received payment because he had written them a postdated check to obtain the move-in permit. Several subcontractors who placed liens against the property were never paid. Neither the builder was paid any funds out of the last draw.

Therefore, the builder was furious. He told us he had not charged us enough to build the home from the beginning and had shorted himself thousands of dollars, which was not our fault. Only the county would have gotten paid from those funds if we had not called and asked the bank to hold the last check. He would have paid none of those subcontractors, and they would have placed liens against the property, and we would've been responsible for paying them.

As a result of the house not being completed when we were promised, we had to move from the apartment. The six months the owners had given us were up. Consequently, we had to move into a hotel for two weeks. Therefore, we deducted the cost of being in the hotel for two weeks from the remaining funds. Also, the builder had left all kinds of debris outside. It was when Hurricane Andrew came through and there was a mess we had to clean up. And, for that reason, we charged the builder for labor for loading, discarding the trash, and dumping fees. The cost was deducted from the remaining funds the bank was holding from the draw.

A very stressful ordeal

In addition, there was much-unfinished work to be completed. The builder ended up placing a lien against our property. I am curious about what good that did. When we called him concerning the issues, he'd tell us, "Sue me; you would be suing my business, not me." He was a very arrogant man. One day, backing out of the driveway, I heard a loud sound that came from something that had fallen. I got out of my car and walked towards the front door of our house. At the front door entrance, the soffit above, as you step out, had fallen from the ceiling. It would have hit me in the head if I had walked out of the front door instead of the garage.

I decided to call the county to file a complaint against the builder. After giving the county the builder's name, they looked up our permit and said, "He's not your builder." So, I gave them the builder's name again. They repeated, "He's not your builder." Your builder's name is Mr. Blank. At that time, we found out he was using someone else's contractor's license. The person's license he was using was a well-known contractor. His father had been the president of one of the banks where I had been employed.

Once we informed the builder of our knowledge of him using someone else's license, his attitude changed. The builder whose permit he was using; once we contacted him and explained what was going on, then everything not completed was completed. The builder whose license was being used reconstructed the fallen soffit in the entryway of our front door. The initial builder really built us a lovely home, but we had many headaches along the way. He took shortcuts and started using cheap materials after realizing he had underestimated the cost. Therefore, it was a very stressful ordeal dealing with the builder.

We later found out he was building another home for someone else at the same time and would use funding from one house to get work done at the other house. This is what was causing the delay in the building. Unfortunately, we were told the other home was never completed, and in this case, you are still responsible for paying the loan. Therefore, you must be very careful when building to do your research. Make sure the builder/contractors are reputable. Our case was not an isolated one. There are unscrupulous builders out there. We were one step ahead of this builder. Thanks to God, he had his hedge of protection around us.

Finally, we moved into our second home in March 1993. The building process for us was a nightmare. A few of the liens were never paid. The subcontractors that placed the liens on the property have one year to enforce it; if not, they are unenforceable. They were never implemented. We had our pastor come and bless our new home.

Our friends who told us about the land purchased an acre in a subdivision a street over and built a home. They have since sold that house and purchased another, and sold it. They now live in

Georgia and have bought and sold numerous times. We can't keep up with them, but they are doing great.

A tragedy

In October of 1998, we had these renters whom the young lady had gotten behind on her rent and was asked to move out. She had two beautiful little girls, a two and a three-year-old. After being given proper notice, she was refusing to leave. Finally, she was supposed to move out on a Monday, but she did not. The following Tuesday morning, she got up to walk her two kids to school at Head Start. A lady driving home from work ran off the road after dosing off and killed the three of them. *A time to mourn,* (Eccles. 3:4b KJV).

It was a very tragic thing to happen to them. We had stopped by the house about two weeks before the accident and met the two little girls. They were adorable. It could be said; that if the mother had moved on Monday when she had planned, they would still be alive. But it was their time. What are the odds of that happening at that particular time on that specific morning in that particular spot? It could be said; that it was destined. They were here for a season, and their season was over. It was at that time we decided to sell the rental property, and we did. So, in December 1998, we sold the first home we had purchased. *To every thing, there is a season,* (Eccles. 3:1 KJV).

Joined my brother's church

In 1998, my husband and I joined my brother's church that he and his second wife started. We were faithful attendees. Bible study we attended off and on, but we were very involved in the church. We loved the members. Reliable tithe payers, we were as well. As a young girl, my grandmother taught me about paying tithes to the church. Most people do not believe in it because they see so much wrongdoing with finances in the church.

One of my responsibilities in the church at one time was handling finances. My brother chose me for that role because I had worked in banking for so long, and he trusted me. It was dual control, meaning someone always handled the finances along with me. I would have never wanted that responsibility to be on me alone. Not that it would keep someone from accusing you of wrongdoing anyway. People will blame you for misconduct and attach everything you own to your duties of handling the finances. It's how people think and because we are quick to accuse someone of wrongdoing.

Going forth, paying tithe is very important in the church. *Honour the LORD with thy substance, And with the first fruits of all thine increase:* (Prov. 3:9 KJV). You may hear someone say, God doesn't need money. God doesn't need money. We are God's instruments while here on earth. He is not here, so he uses us to do the work. Therefore, we are to pay tithes for whatever is required to operate the church and to keep those doors open for anyone who needs to hear the word of God. So, consequently, if anything is going on with the funding that is not right, we have to trust God to deal with it. We must do our part as faithful stewards of God.

You will be blessed according to your faithfulness. Since our church closed its doors, we haven't been attending a church or paying tithes. We will pay ten percent of our income when we join a church again. It has been ingrained in me. I am sure those faithful tithers can attest to gaining rather than losing when paying their ten-percent contribution.

We enjoyed the things we did for our community while in the church. We would have clothes and food giveaways. For Thanksgiving, my husband and I would reach out to Publix, Winn-

Dixie, Walmart, and PepsiCo for donations. PepsiCo would donate drinks. Winn-Dixie and Publix would donate turkeys and a gift card to purchase food.

We would ask different members to cook the turkeys, macaroni and cheese, collard greens, rice, green beans, mashed potatoes, cornbread, and deserts and feed the homeless on Thanksgiving Day. It was so rewarding to provide food to the homeless. Some of the members would be there and enjoy the fellowship as well. We had some terrific times coming together. We had many people join the church; they would come and go for whatever reason. We enjoyed being involved in the church. *To every thing, there is a season, (Eccles. 3:1 KJV).*

Prayed and trusted God

My husband and I experienced marital problems during our marriage. I will not go through the details, but we had our issues. Marriage is not easy. Therefore, I moved out in 2002 for a year and moved back in 2003 before the passing of our son.

Then in 2006, I filed for a divorce. The divorce was my decision and was because of me. My husband's attorney filed an appeal. So, my attorney informed me that I would have to pay her another twenty-two hundred dollars due to the requests. Hence, it was an indication to me that God did not want us to divorce. I was angry, but I needed to take heed. If it were for us to get divorced, we would be divorced. God disapproved of it, and I recognized the signs. I would've regretted it.

I knew my husband had been praying and trusting God. God answered his prayers and worked it out. We forgave one another. My husband is a good man. We both have our faults, but we love one another. Again, marriage is not easy. We have to work at it to make it successful. We are easily ready to give up and think the grass may be greener on the other side and find out after it's too late that it is not. He has always been a family man; providing for his household and being there for us. Always supporting and encouraging me. So, that to me is appreciated. A man who also has much wisdom to share with me through the years that have helped me to grow and become a better person, as well as, a man that has much faith and much patience.

Helped shape him

My husband continues to mention to me how his junior varsity high school basketball coach helped shape him into a young man in his sophomore year. Because of his facial expressions when he played basketball, the coach could see it on his face when he disagreed, was angry, disappointed, or was frustrated because of a bad call. The coach would tell him, never let them see you sweat. Look at the opposing team and smile. Therefore, it is hard for me to imagine my husband being no other way than he is now. Calm and, easygoing he has always been. But he says he has not always been that way. The opposite is me; he has to calm me down. Opposites do attract. It takes a lot to get him angry.

He talks about how playing basketball in school opened him up to many opportunities he would not have experienced if he had not been playing. Therefore, he was able to travel to many places and meet many people. Being out with the recruiters, they would eat at upscale restaurants, stay in five-star hotels, visit beaches, go jet skiing, and ride fast ski boats, he would say. He also had the opportunity to hang out with other potential players. There were exciting experiences he had. His mother, he said, never came to see him play basketball, and he had one sister to attend one of his games at his high school.

A friend, he said, about five years older than him, took him under his wing and taught him a lot about basketball. So, he looked up to this person like a father and spent much time around him. His friend's wife would cook, and he would spend time at their house and eat sometimes. This friend allowed him to drive his car and would encourage him when he was around him. But, when he left Ft. Myers and went to Mississippi to college, they lost contact.

Years after we were married, my husband took me to Ft. Myers and visited his friend at his house. This was when I met his friend and his wife. His wife impressed me when his friend asked her to cook us something to eat, and she went right into the kitchen and fried some chicken, and prepared cabbage, rice, and cornbread. I was hungry, and it was yummy. Since that time, I think about his friend and his wife and being at their home every time I cook cabbage. After that, his friend would always stop and visit between his trips from Ft. Myers to Clearwater, Fl. His friend's mother lived in Clearwater, and he always traveled from Ft. Myers to Clearwater to visit her.

His friend divorced and remarried

Eventually, his friend and his wife divorced. He started bringing a lady friend from Clearwater by the house, and we would do things together. We would go yearly to the Clearwater Jazz Festival and so forth. We enjoyed their company. They attended our daughter's wedding, and he caught the garter belt when the groom tossed it and placed it on his lady friend's leg. They were married in May of the following year. Since that time, we may have seen them several times afterward. Whenever my husband called him and left a message, there would be no response.

He had never been that way towards my husband before. They had known each other since my husband was a teen. Therefore, we assumed his wife no longer wanted to befriend us. She was a much younger woman, and we assume that as long as she was dating him, she did what was needed to keep him. Nevertheless, we sent a card saying if there's anything we did to offend them, please forgive us. It was never acknowledged whether they received the card or not. It was odd because he and my husband had been so close.

However, the last time we saw his friend and his wife was at my husband's boss's funeral, who had passed away from cancer. My husband had introduced his friend to his boss before his death, and they had become friends. We all had gone out together a few times. We were cordial when we saw them at the funeral, but we never heard from them again. My husband continued to call and leave messages, and his friend would not respond. However, we have accepted that we were friends only for a season. "Everything has its time."

Before my husband's boss passed away, they had become good friends. My husband would say that his boss was a person that puts up much bark. He was a very intelligent and knowledgeable man. My husband would always tell me he and I were alike because we were under the same zodiac sign. We were both Taurus the bull; direct, straightforward, to the point when we speak, and stubborn. Before his passing, my husband said his boss would put up this persona for people to keep their distance, but once you get past that and get to know him, he was kind, loving, and giving. My husband gives me credit for being the same way. He says, I care too much and try to do too much for people.

A stronger Relationship

My husband loves basketball and continues to play in a league. Therefore, he has plenty of friends and acquaintances from playing basketball. Also, he made plenty of friends while working at his job, and is a person that can go anywhere and make acquaintances. A conversation is something he can start with anyone.

At this time, our relationship is stronger and better than ever. We have grown and are much more mature and understand how important marriage and family are, even though we still get on each other nerves. But we continue to be there for one another, enjoying life and vacations with family. Like this trip to Tennessee again in 2016 with our grandkids. We stayed at the Westgate Smokey Mountain Resort & Spa in Gatlinburg. Loving the great Smokey Mountains; we even got to see a little snow. The scenery was so beautiful and breathtaking. Our daughter, granddaughter, grandson, and I went horseback riding at Sugarland's Riding Stables, and I thought I was going to have a heart attack. It was the most frightening experience I have ever had. I felt like that horse was going to trip, and we both will fall down the mountain and die. My heart was beating so fast. It seemed as though the horse ride would never end. Therefore, you couldn't get back to the stable and off the horse fast enough.

We stayed in a cabin in Pigeon Forge; it was like being at home. You had everything you needed and more. We visited many attractions. At one of the restaurants, we enjoyed the catfish. It was so delicious. At least three times, we have vacationed there. While there, we toured many places. We loved the scenery. It is breathtaking looking over the mountains.

Our family trip to Myrtle Beach, South Carolina, was also exciting. Walking along the beach and eating, we just loved it. It was beautiful looking out over the water. Our daughter, granddaughter, and great-grandson were brave and took a ride on a helicopter. They were so excited.

My husband and I have traveled to Savanna, Georgia, many times and we love it there. Savannah is very historical, and the scenery is also breathtaking. The manicured parks with the old oak trees are beautiful. They have trolleys that take you around the city and give you the history. We would stay at the Embassy Suites on Oglethorpe Avenue, where we could walk to Riverwalk and surrounding attractions. Along the Riverwalk, there are plenty of stores to shop at and restaurants to eat along the river. We would hang out at the park, where there would be many people, live bands, and plenty of places to eat, drink and be merry. There are places to go for every occasion.

We have gone on cruises with our daughter and granddaughter and also alone. On our last cruise to Nassau and Freeport Bahamas in 2020, we celebrated our 40th Anniversary. We had a fantastic time. We were truly thankful to be celebrating 40 years together. God is good.

Retired after 34 years

My husband worked at his job for many years. He started as a lab helper and ended up as a Senior Technician. In his role as a senior technician, he performed various jobs. Therefore, being top quality, his position required traveling all over the plant. He gained much respect from the workers, staff, and vendors the company used due to his knowledge and experience.

During his years of service at the plant, he received many awards and honors. He learned a lot which allowed him to move up with the company. With his moving up, he would provide training, attend meetings and go out to eat with upper management. As a liaison, he often had to travel to different vendor plants to inspect new designs and materials. In addition, he was always a part of new development projects. Everyone thought he was a manager because he was respected among his peers.

Through the years, he ran into people who did not have his best interest and tried to get him fired, but because of the respect he had formed with various people, they could not do so. So, my husband continued to do his job, and God removed all those obstacles. Those people were no longer around for one reason or another. Nevertheless, he retired at the beginning of 2015 after working for 34 years. *To everything, there is a season, and a time for every purpose under the heaven:* (Eccles. 3:1 NKJV).

Chapter Ten

Our Son

A Typical adventurous kid

A time to be born, (Eccles. 3:2 KJV). December 1, 1971, at 7:40 a.m. At a young age, I gave birth to our son, of whom my husband is not the father. As a typical adventurous kid growing up, someone gave him a nickname that everyone knew him by. Although, I never referred to him by that name. Considered quiet, he had many friends and acquaintances.

His school years became tough for him because he struggled with learning. Therefore, it appeared obvious traditional learning was not for him. He'd been enrolled in a private Christian school for a short time, but he did not fit in, and neither did he like it. He ended up back in regular school and we

enrolled him in art school on the weekends because
of his interest in art.

At twelve years old, he played for the Pop
Warner Football Program and received a certificate
of achievement award; and received a certificate of
participation award for the 4-H/Tropicana Public
Speaking Program; and at 13 years old, he took part
in the Manatee Youth Festival of Art. Because of
his success in track, he won several track and field
awards.

Dropped out of high school

He dropped out of high school in the 10th
grade. He started attending a vocational school for a
while for cosmetology and barbering but stopped.
He'd been a fantastic barber who loved cutting hair.
Even though he did not have his license, he would
cut hair for many neighborhood friends. Artistic
designs he'd put within haircuts for those that
desired it. He would apply perms to his wife's hair
as well as cut and style it. And would apply perms
to my hair. He'd advise me on what lipstick to wear.
He told me, "Mom, that lipstick color is too light for
your skin type, you need to wear darker lipstick
colors." I agreed. Darker colors made a difference.
He loved doing things with his hands. We'd given
him this CD player/recorder one Christmas, and he

took it apart. His stepdad got upset with him, but he put it back together as though it had never been taken apart. He enjoyed repairing electronics. Everyone is not good in the books, but God will give us other gifts. We all have them whether we recognize them or use them.

Married in 1993

In 1990, his girlfriend became pregnant at 15 and, his age at the time was 19. They had a healthy little girl, our granddaughter, born on January 24, 1991. Another young lady gave birth to a son from him the same year giving me a grandson. Initially, the mother thought someone else fathered him. Our son believed all along that he was the father and would have me check on him when he was in jail. He and his daughter's mother married in August 1993, and they gave birth to our second granddaughter in 1997.

His wife had another child in December 1999. She named the baby after our son, but our son did not father the child. A guy who believed he was the child's parent went to court and took a paternity test and it was proven he was the father. The young man then requested the court to change the child's name to his, for which they granted him the request. The father took custody of his son and raised him because of my ex-daughter-in-law's drug addiction. The situation destroyed our son, and later he filed for a divorce.

In and out of jail

He started going in and out of jail after 1992. As I was told, when he started selling drugs, his wife began using them. This is when their marriage began failing. His wife could not battle that spirit of drugs even until this day. Therefore, I ask all my readers to please pray that God will deliver all from addictions and those suffering from mental health issues; strengthen their minds and body and make them all whole again; and give them the faith to believe that He can heal their bodies, in Jesus' name. However, our son struggled with his usage of alcohol and drugs. They had sentenced him to one year and four months in prison for drugs in 2001. While in and out of jail, he discovered his talent for drawing. He would write and send beautiful pictures he'd sketched and tell me it seemed like God would take his hands and move them during his drawing. He appeared gifted and talented in art.

A typical Friday evening

After they released him from prison in July 2002, he met a young woman and moved in with her. A typical Friday evening, it seemed. My husband had asked me if I wanted to go out or do something. He wanted us to get out of the house. But I just did not want to go anywhere. My son ended up calling me. We were having a casual conversation, so it appeared. My son told me he cut this guy's hair, and he'd been cooking. His stepdad had been there earlier and gotten a haircut. He said my son seemed happy and told him they were expecting to have guests come over.

We ended our conversation, and he called me back again. He must have called me about three times that evening. Therefore, I asked him, "Why do you keep calling me," he answered, "Because I love my mama." I told him, "I love you too." He continued to talk as though he'd been drinking. He continued telling me how much he loved me and was just talking.

However, I asked him to put his lady friend, whom he lived with, on the telephone. When she got on the phone, I asked her if our son had been drinking, and she answered, "No, ma'am," but she lied. I asked his stepdad to get on the telephone and talk with him. I learned later that in his conversation with his stepdad, his lady friend's brother and his friend left this guy at their apartment, and our son was not comfortable with him being there.

Suspected something

My husband said my son shared with him, he felt the guy seemed disrespectful. While his lady friend's brother and his friend left to buy more drinks, they left this person there, with whom our son was not familiar, playing a video game. How he ends up at the apartment as told to me; her brother and his friend, who knew the guy, picked him up while walking along the road. They then invited him to come along to his sister's apartment. Our son suspected something may have been going on between this guy and his lady friend.

While on the telephone with his stepdad, his stepdad told him he might need to step outside and try to calm down. He also told him; that he would come to the apartment if he did not start talking differently. His stepdad then returned the phone back to me. Our son must have placed the phone down but did not hang it up. Therefore, I could barely hear my son and his lady friend because the sound was muffled. I heard a thumping sound, and thought, "Did he hit his lady friend?" Unclear, I could not determine what was happening. Continuing to call my son's name for him to pick the phone back up; he never did, so I hung the phone up.

From then on, I dialed the telephone number back, and the line continued to be busy; because the phone was off the hook on their end. His lady friend called me back a few minutes later and said, "You need to get here. There is blood everywhere." I asked, "What do you mean there is blood everywhere?" "What happened?" She said, "I don't know."

I knew that meant he would not make it

I told my husband he needed to go to their place to see what was happening. When my husband got there, he called me and told me that the EMTs said it would be useless for them to fly our son to Bayfront because of him going in and out. They would instead take him to Manatee Memorial Hospital because he needed immediate care. I knew whatever had taken place in that apartment, my son would not make it.

A time to die; (Eccles. 3:2 NKJV). On the late evening of August 15, 2003, he had lost too much blood. Our son was murdered. *A time to weep;*

(Eccles. 3:4a NKJV). A day and time I will never forget.

We had advised him, "If you are going to drink, drink at home." At home drinking, and the person visiting his home took his life. His lady friend's brother and his friend picked up this person and brought him to his sister's house. This guy ends up stabbing our son to death. Our son's friends he grew up with knew his normal behavior was quiet, but they also realized that when he would drink alcohol, his personality would change, and he could be the opposite; talkative, bold, and aggressive. This is why we advised him to drink at home.

When our son placed the telephone down, he must have walked over and hit the guy, which was the wrong decision. The guy came there with an ice pick in his pocket and stabbed him repeatedly. Why did he have an ice pick in his pocket? Why did her brother and his friend leave him there? The young man's age was 21, and our son was 32.

Man, I give up

A big guy and our son was slender. He told the guy, "Man, I give up." He'd broken his arm about a year earlier and it had not healed. I suppose the liqueur provided him with a false sense of strength. It devastated me to hear that. It broke my heart.

Something else that broke my heart was that his lady friend has a daughter around the same age as his daughter. They were around twelve years old at the time of his death. Her daughter was at the house during this time, and he kept calling her name, telling her he was dying. That's a traumatizing experience for anyone. It breaks my heart to know she had to experience that situation. Our granddaughter had moved to their apartment with them, but she had spent the weekend at her aunt's house. It was traumatic for her to learn her father had passed. A relative visiting us after his death told me she needed counseling by the look in her eyes, but I never got her that counseling.

My husband and I had been raising my granddaughter. She and I had moved to an apartment complex during my separation from my husband for a year, but I had moved back home before his death. After his release from prison in July 2002, a year before his death, he came to my apartment one night and told me how he felt growing up. His words were, "Mom, you showed me love by buying me things. I needed you to hug and kiss me like a mama." An affectionate mother, I am not. He also told me how much he loved me and always tried to please me.

A time to mend

We had a long mother-and-son talk. *A time to tear and a time to mend, a time to be silent and a time to speak,* (Eccles. 3:7 NIV). I told him I was sorry for not giving him what he felt he needed. I explained to him it was not my intention to have a child at such a young age, and that I did not understand how to be a mother being a child myself. I also let him know why it had been difficult for me to be affectionate. My mother always shied away when we tried to hug and kiss her. She couldn't take it. However, she wasn't nasty about it. I do not recall my grandmother showing affection either, but they both loved us. We learn the ways and habits of those that come before us.

I was not the best mother to my son when I was younger. When my sister would come home from school, I would leave him home with her to babysit. My sister said she would look around, and I would be gone; gone trying to be a teenager. So, when I became an adult, I tried to make up for how I treated him by buying him everything, but he needed more. God allowed me and my son to clear

the air before he died. For everything, there is a
purpose.

Tears started coming down

My husband and I had gone on a trip to the
Smokey Mountains in Tennessee around August 1,
2003, two weeks before he died. We had planned to
leave early on a Friday morning. Not satisfied with
my hair, I drove to the Beauty Academy, where our
son had been attending barber school. Going on the
spur of the moment to get my hair done before
leaving on a trip is something I had never done
before. For everything, there is a purpose. I do not
believe it just happened.

The owner of the academy, when I told her our
son had been taking classes there, talked on and on
about how much she admired him and how he was a
great artist. She said, "He talked about you all the
time." This lady talked continuously, telling me
how much my son loved me. She showed me this
picture he drew of her granddaughter, and tears
started coming down from her eyes. He had drawn a
magnificent drawing of her granddaughter's picture.

I had been destined to go to that academy
before leaving to go on that vacation for a reason.
God knew what we would have to face two weeks

147

after returning. I had a fantastic conversation with the owner of the academy. Therefore, it was mainly my conversation while traveling to Tennessee on how strange it was to be prompted to go to that academy. God is good! God had His way of bringing me through the death of my child. "Everything has its time." Before he died, he knew how much we loved him, and I was made aware of how much he loved me. God gave me peace with my son's death. The peace that surpasses all understanding.

Before going to Tennessee, I would drive to this bridge, sit, stare out at the water, and pray. I did this for several weeks. God was preparing me during this time. I did not realize why I was there, but God allowed me to gain peace for what I would endure. God knows everything before it happens.

Also, the night he passed away, my daughter and I got into the car to drive to the hospital. When opening the door to step into the car, there were these envelopes between the seat and the console. When I pulled out the envelopes, I realized several insurance payments had fallen from other payments I mailed several weeks earlier. One payment was the life insurance for our son.

Somehow I missed making the payment, which is something I rarely do. Therefore, this payment that slipped between the seats was a payment for two months. It was an omen. *A time for every purpose under heaven:* (Eccles. 3:1 NKJV). I had been getting in and out of the car every day, and I did not discover those envelopes until the night of his death. It was God making me aware that He is with me. Therefore, I made sure I mailed those envelopes the next day.

However, I called the insurance company and explained the situation. It appeared they would try to get out of paying the policy because it was late, but they should have been able to see that I had been paying the policy on time in previous years. Also, they could see the date on the check as well as the check made out for the two months.

I told them how they advertise for someone to take out a policy for their loved ones because you never know when death will come, and you want the insurance to bury them. It was that time for my family. God had allowed me to find those envelopes. I am humbled when saying this; the insurance company paid the policy. Everything has its time.

I can't question his death

I can't question his death. If God was not ready for him, he would be here. My husband and I understand this because one evening, on a Friday night, we were out riding. While stopped at a light, this car crossed us traveling west. We began noticing the vehicle swerving along the road. I told my husband something was wrong with that driver, so we followed him. The driver continued bobbing as we crossed another light. Then we were coming up to a third light, and as the car slowly approached, we pulled up beside him and noticed his head slumping in the car.

I told my husband we needed to do something. My husband put our car in park, immediately got out of it, and into this person's car. I hurriedly took over our vehicle. He quickly pushed the guy over to take over the wheel of his car, and the vehicle continued moving under the red light. Thank God he had cleared the way for this because there were no cars coming either way. The young man promptly awakened and asked my husband what was going on. My husband explained to him what we witnessed driving behind him.

Everything Has Its Time

Supposedly he was on his way home; he told my husband. My husband asked him, "Where do you live?" and he told my husband where he lived. Oddly, he lived in the direction he had been coming from. He then told my husband about being tired and falling asleep. My husband drove him home while I followed them.

What my husband did that night you would consider heroic. He saved that young man's life and risked his own. We believed God had us go in that direction that evening to save that young man's life. It was not his time to go. We also believe that if it was not our son's time to go, God would not have allowed my son's lady friend, brother, and friend to pick that young man up, and bring him to their house that evening. *"Everything has its time."*

In a better place

Our son struggled to get his life together for his family. He loved them, and it seemed to take a toll on him to see what his wife had become. I am sure he blamed himself for her being on drugs, therefore; he'd been dealing with a lot mentally and would always tell me, "Mama Artists do not live long." An aspiring artist he strived to be. A few weeks before he passed away, he gave me some of his drawings, and one was of Jay-Z from his CD cover, Jay-Z,

151

The Blueprint. He told me, "Mama, you will figure out what to do with them." I'm sorry, I did not know what to do with them. Three of them are framed and on our wall. I chose one drawing and used it on the cover of his obituary. Before his passing, I'd created a portfolio of his sketches. He told me to give it to his son, my grandson, and I honored that request.

He is now in a better place. I believe God freed him of his struggles because nothing happens unless God allows it. He has a way of freeing us from all of our troubles. He now has peace. He did not suffer long because of being in and out of consciousness. I forgave the young man that took his life when it happened. He would have wanted me to do that. That's my son. He loved people and would give someone his last. The guy turned himself in on that Monday after he committed the crime. During his trial, he testified our son had been very hospitable to him before the stabbing. They released him from prison on July 27, 2021, after serving 18 years for murder.

A time to mourn, (Eccles. 3:4b KJV). We held his funeral services on August 23, 2003, at a local church where my second oldest brother gave his eulogy. Before his death, he had given his life to Christ. *A time to dance;* (Eccles. 3:4b KJV).

To every thing, there is a season and a time to every purpose under the heaven: (Eccles. 3:1. KJV).

Chapter Eleven

Our Daughter

Elementary and middle school years

After being born on March 25, 1982, at 3:33 pm., our lovely daughter kept us busy as the years passed by, taking her back and forth to daycares as we both went to work daily. She attended elementary school in Bradenton from 1987 through 1993. Her father would call her a little militant because she stood up for fellow students' rights.

She was a quiet girl, but she always spoke up when needed. She received her share of First Place and Honorable Mention Track and Field awards. An award for Outstanding Reader, Certificate of Participation from Tropicana 4-H Public Speaking, Certificate of Honor for the 4-H Speech Contest, Recognition for Super Student, Classroom Hero for Outstanding Effort, School Safety Patrol Award of

Merit, Library Service Award for Media Helper and one-year Perfect Attendance Award. She was very involved in many activities during her elementary school years.

She attended a local middle school in Bradenton from 1994 until 1996. During those years, she was involved more in attending the Barbizon School of Modeling in Tampa, Florida. Barbizon is an international modeling and acting school that provides modeling, acting, and personal development, including self-confidence, proper posture, photo movement, etiquette, makeup application, and runway.

She was not as involved in middle school as in elementary school. Our daughter was always timid. Attending Barbizon helped her somewhat grow out of her timidity. The school helped her with her self-confidence, proper posture, etiquette, and all. We kept her dressed nicely, and she was always a pretty girl, loving clothes and makeup.

Devastating years

Then came those high school years from 1997 until the year 2000. It started when she was in the ninth and tenth grades. Those years were devastating for her. To this day, she does not enjoy talking about her high school years. First, there were two girls with whom she had no involvement, but they were harassing her for no reason. One day, she came home and told me those girls planned to jump on her the next day.

That day, January 13, 1998, I made it a point at 7:30 a.m. to go to her high school to alert the school liaison officer; the word was out that those two girls were to jump our daughter. So, this person called my daughter to the office and began counseling her as though she was the instigator. Then, after leaving the school, 45 minutes later, this liaison officer called for me to pick up our daughter for fighting. The two girls set a fire alarm to distract the teacher's attention while jumping on her. Then, the school suspends her for two days for defending herself from these girls.

Fight was deliberate

The school placed the blame on her, saying she violated school rules. After going to the school to warn them, she was still at fault for trying to defend herself. She told us that there were no teachers anywhere when she looked around. What was she supposed to do? The school admitted the fight was deliberate, and the girls had set off the fire alarm.

The two girls were stepsisters, and because of the last name of one of them, the family was known to the school for their outstanding athletic abilities; therefore, the school would do nothing. The situation could have been avoided if the school liaison officer to whom I reported had interceded by talking with those girls after I left his office that morning.

It was said that several students and adults had complained about high-profile athletes and their families getting away with incidents at the school. They set up a meeting at the office with the school resource officer, the liaison officer, the two girls, their mother/stepmother, our daughter, and me. The two girls were so disrespectful and rude in front of the mother/stepmother. They commented they did not like her and also said other ugly things about her. Our daughter stood up and said, "I will not sit here and let these girls talk about me like this." She walked out of the room while the meeting was being held. I did not blame her. It was not right because the mother/stepmother was allowing it.

Being bullied

The following school year, she started having issues avoiding going to certain classes because a girl two years older was bullying her. We had to transfer her to another school on the west side of town. She continued to go there until it became too difficult to get her back and forth. She experienced some very tough high school years that were traumatizing to her. What she encountered during high school affected her so much that she did not want to attend college.

However, she did graduate high school in the year 2000. To this day, she does not like to talk about her high school years.

She became pregnant

In 2002, at 21, she became pregnant. One night while lying in bed, she did not feel her baby moving during her eighth month of pregnancy. She had this device that would monitor her heartbeat. This night, she was not hearing her heartbeat. So she called the hospital, and they had her drink orange juice to make her move. She still did not move. She did not tell anyone but became afraid and drove herself to the hospital at three or four o'clock in the morning.

At the hospital, our granddaughter was being monitored. They discovered her heartbeat was faint. They did an emergency C-section, and she was told that our grandbaby would not have made it if she had not come to the hospital. Her biblical cord was wrapped around her neck. That was why she remained still and had not been moving. God is always looking out for us. Our fourth grandchild was born on March 12, 2003.

On Monday, August 18, 2003, three days after the death of our son, and is also her grandmother's birthday, she started working at this job and has continued her employment there. Until she departs, I will always remember how many years it's been by the number of years our son has been deceased.

Beautiful wedding

She met this guy; and because of some of his actions, her father and I told her he was not the one for her, but she was in love. They were married in 2008 and had a beautiful church wedding and reception. Their wedding was at her uncle's church, and he officiated it. The colors were lavender, purple, and white. It was a lovely wedding. Our daughter was excited to be married.

But, because of marital issues, they divorced in 2014. Then came the shock when she learned he had remarried in two months.

It was devastating to her daughter, our granddaughter. Her stepfather just walked out of her life. So, she has been going through so much because she thought she loved him more than her biological father. He had been in her life since she was around three years old and left when she was going into middle school. With her stepfather leaving her; her natural father not being consistent in her life; it has been damaging to her teenage years. People do not realize their selfish decisions affect everyone they are involved with, and their decisions can leave lifetime damage to someone's life.

At the end of my employment with a bank in 2012, someone came in with this little puppy. He was going to be dropped off at someone's home that had purchased it. There were more puppies in their car. They were beautiful Pomeranians mixed with Shih Tzu puppies. After seeing how excited we were about the one they brought in, they got the others for us to see. They were so adorable. The branch manager and I fell in love with them.

I asked my daughter if they would be interested in me getting one for our granddaughter. She had been asking for a dog. My daughter approved of me getting the dog for her. It was to be a family dog whenever they moved. The branch manager and I purchased one, and my daughter named him Milo.

Milo helped her heal

Everyone fell in love with Milo. You know, God can see and knows what lies ahead of us. We can't see ahead, but God knows everything. There is a purpose for everything. Her ex-husband left Milo behind as well. My daughter told me that little Milo helped her get through and heal from the hurt of her divorce. Our little Milo showed and gave her the unconditional love she needed. It seems my purpose for being at that job was to buy that puppy. I worked one year for that bank and left right after purchasing him and had no clue he was to serve a purpose.

God said he would never leave us nor forsake us. He brought our daughter through, even though it was tough on her, but God did it. He allowed her to love her husband for a season. His story in her life ended. If it were not to be, God would not have allowed it. So, we wished nothing but the best for her ex-husband and his wife. But, we have since heard... they have divorced.

We are proud of our daughter and how God helped her handle the situation. She is a very classy and sophisticated woman who carries herself with dignity. She is a good woman and I'm not just saying it because she is our daughter. Desiring to get married again; she is trusting God to send her the right man. In the meantime, she is trying to live her life. She was awarded her Associate of Arts degree in 2020 and is strongly considering continuing her education. Even though she has experienced some difficult challenges, she seems to remain resilient because of her trust in God, and because of His blessings on her life. Everything has its time. *To Every thing there is a season, and a time for every purpose under the heaven: (Eccles. 3:1 KJV).*

Chapter Twelve

Employment Challenges

Being an ambitious person, it was my nature to continue to look for opportunities for advancement. My first entry-level job was with the city in our town from February 1977 until June 1981. The job with the city was a government job that offered wonderful benefits and a pension. When hired, I had been out of high school for a couple of years. Being young, you do not consider benefits and pensions.

Working at city hall in any county can be a secure job if you are fortunate to get hired. To advance there, you have to be patient and willing to wait until someone retires to move up unless they create a position for you. In my entry-level job I held, the employees would only stay for a short time because there was no opportunity for advancement. Someone would have to retire, resign or pass away in upper-level positions for you to advance, and one would rarely quit their positions. It was just a temporary job for most until they finished college or another opportunity came. I met a lot of good people in the position. One co-worker worked while attending school to become a lawyer, like most of her family.

After getting married at the end of 1979, I resigned to move to another county. Then, I returned to work there in June 1981 after things did not go as planned with our move. I later applied and got hired at the bank next door. Therefore, I resigned again. I'd worked a total of four years at the city at their front counter.

At the bank next door, it was my first teller position and where my teller training began. Being a teller was enjoyable. I loved counting money, and there were opportunities for advancement. However, my experience let me know it was not where I wanted to continue my employment.

Surprise audit

One morning before getting started, the head teller and the assistant head teller gave me a surprise audit. Then, during the audit, they discovered that five hundred dollars were missing from my drawer after they counted the money. They wrote me up for being five hundred dollars short. Then the following day, when I'd counted my money before starting the day, my drawer was five hundred dollars over.

How did the money reappear? How did that make me look? Someone who had access to that key tried to make it look like I'd taken the money and returned it. It was to make it appear I was a dishonest person. The question is, what would have been next? So, my employment with them was very short, from June 1981 until December 1981.

Company dissolved

An ex-coworker from the City Hall informed me of a receptionist position open at this chemical corporation where her daughter worked in the office. I'd applied for the position and they hired me. At the time, I was pregnant, and a few months later, gave birth to our baby girl, born on March 25, 1982.

Chapter Twelve: Employment Challenges

So, the ladies in the office gave me a baby shower and provided me with beautiful gifts for our healthy daughter. Then, while on maternity leave, the company laid-off employees, giving me six months' severance pay. The company later dissolved, and I was out of a job for several months until another door opened.

Given too much back

Early in my career, working for several banks as a teller or head teller was the job that kept me employed. Some encounters are difficult to forget, like giving someone three thousand dollars too much back in cash. This happened when two crew leaders came into the bank to cash their payroll checks to pay the workers at a tomato plant. There were many tomato packing houses in Palmetto.

On this particular Friday, my drawer was three thousand dollars short after I'd cashed out the check for the payroll. I can't recall the exact payroll amount, but the crew leaders would always request so much in each denomination. So, after realizing my drawer was short, and reviewing my tape calculations, my error was determined. It was apparent. I'm sure the two crew leaders realized the mistake and knew it was too much when I handed them the money. The bank was very familiar with the tomato company. So someone from the bank contacted them and spoke with the two crew leaders, and they denied receiving too much money.

However, the assistant branch manager who would assist us when we were busy on the teller line with large deposits; told the head teller she confused me when giving me money ordered from the vault. She had told me the cash vault was out of large bills, then she came and gave me large bills. The exchange had nothing to do with my error, but I appreciated her for trying to cover it up for me. An excellent teller I've always been, regardless of that error. God is an exceptional God and looked out for me.

Caught red-handed

Despite that, they later promoted me to a head teller and moved me to one of their new locations in the Financial Center. A well-known local family bought the bank in Palmetto around 1986. The Financial Center was a beautiful place. I'd been proud to go to work there. Then, one day leaving to go to lunch and returned abruptly after forgetting something, my two tellers had gotten caught red-handed trying to open my drawer. They were trying to see if I'd left my drawer unlocked. That was an awkward moment. So, it was never determined what their intentions were. Whatever it was, it wasn't good.

As mentioned earlier, I continued seeking job opportunities. In 1988, went to work for a credit union and worked there for one year as a part-time teller while attending college. Most of the credit union customers were school employees. Being a family member of a credit union customer, you could open an account. The credit union would be very busy on teachers' payday. The line would be out the door, therefore, the branch manager would buy groceries and stock the refrigerator with food, so we did not have to leave the building during those busy days for lunch.

Head start program

My next venture was working for Head Start in 1989 as a social services/volunteer specialist. Head Start is a federally funded program to promote school readiness for children three to five years old from low-income families. The program encourages parent involvement through regular visits to the child's home and opportunities for parents to volunteer in the program. Some received free medical and dental care services and healthy meals and snacks.

My position was providing enrollment for the children attending Head Start and assisting families with needed services. My responsibilities also required me to oversee and keep track of volunteers, and to acknowledge them at the Annual Volunteer Tea. The director had started a paying classroom that served 20 children whose parents were over income and did not qualify for the regular Head Start Program. I was responsible for keeping the enrollment at 20 kids and collecting the fees for that program.

There were two directors that I'd had the privilege of working under at different times. Both directors, during their tenures, allowed me to complete my education while working. Therefore, receiving an Associate of Arts degree from Manatee Community College in May 1991. In December 1993, received a B.A. degree in Interdisciplinary Social Sciences from the University of South Florida. Then, after receiving my bachelor's degree, they provided me with a raise.

Attended parent conferences

While working for Head Start, I received much training and took advantage of the opportunities to travel to out-of-state parent conferences. As a result, received awards of appreciation, certificates of achievement, certificates of accomplishments, and certifications in different areas. Also, on Career Development Day, received a Certificate of Merit for Outstanding Accomplishments in Professional Growth. Therefore, always found it to be beneficial to attend parent conferences.

A Parent Conference in Washington, D.C., wherefore, we had the privilege of having the guest speaker Jesse Jackson, a Political Activist, Minister, and Politician. It was an amazing conference, and I learned a lot. It was cold in D.C. when we got there. I remember going to Goodwill to purchase some winter attire before leaving Florida. Coming from Florida and changing over to that type of weather was a shock to my body.

The Parent conference in San Diego, California, was a great experience. We marched down the streets, protesting in this Hispanic neighborhood known for drugs. So we marched down the street saying, "No more drugs," but we were saying it in Spanish. It was exciting. San Diego is a beautiful city.

Also, while in San Diego, we crossed the border to Tijuana, New Mexico. It was certainly a humbling experience. You can't imagine how some of those people have to live. Walking by, you can see dirt floors throughout the tiny houses. Children solicited money to feed their families. Children and adults trying to scam you. So, therefore, you must stay with your group and be careful because they know you are visiting. Everyone was trying to sell something. Some of the stuff you buy in Tijuana could be fake, so you must be careful what you purchase. It was quite an experience.

Once, we were at a conference in Alabama during a weekend, and a couple of us attended a church service that I deemed impressive. Members were being taught at their church that men should head the household and work. Hence, the women are to stay at home and raise their children. They believed in the concept; if we live within our means, we can live off one income. Because as a result, our children suffer from both parents working and being away from home.

We only attended one service years ago. So, unsure how their beliefs hold up for the members today. However, the service with the singing, the worshipping, and how everything was all set up was outstanding. Also, the restaurants we had the pleasure of visiting and trying their foods were delicious. Never will forget that visit. It left me with a pleasurable experience.

Chapter Twelve: Employment Challenges

Then, the Parent conferences in Atlanta were always outstanding. A hotel on Peachtree Street is where we would always stay, and after the conference, myself and a co-worker would put on our sneakers and walk to the underground to look around and shop. We loved it and would have a fantastic time.

Three of us ladies worked together to provide social services at one Head Start location. We worked in a trailer at the back of the Head Start center. There was one of us that worked at another site. For a long time, we did not have a supervisor. Then, the director hired a supervisor to supervise the social services department. We all had reservations about someone coming in and telling us what to do after having our freedom for so long. So, the person the director hired was a lady that had retired from the military.

Other Head Start Programs were already using computers for their caseloads, and we needed to get on board. At first, we were not receptive because we would have to learn something new. We were afraid of change. However, this supervisor, whom I had reservations about, taught me so much about computers. Then, I could consult her whenever I needed advice on work-related or personal situations. She was always there and encouraging me. She had a lot of confidence in me and my abilities. Those two people I worked with, her and my close co-worker, positively made an impact on my professional growth. I thank God for them both and for everything I've learned from them.

Looking to hire an executive director

Head Start set up a table at this event one day, providing information about our program. Our supervisor and I were looking around at other set-ups and gathering information from other tables. We met this man who was the vice president of this bank. He started talking to me about this organization he was involved with that educated first-time homebuyers. He informed me the organization was looking to hire an executive director. So, my supervisor encouraged me to apply based on the potential she saw in me. But, having no experience, I did not think I would qualify.

Later, I contacted the bank's vice president and gathered more details about the job. Based on the job description he provided, it seemed possible I could perform the job duties. Next, the vice president informed me what to do to apply for the position. After applying for the job, they set an interview up for me to meet with the Board president. Met with the Board president and afterward, he set up a meeting with the Board of Directors. Next met with the Board of Directors and they offered me the position. After much consideration and discussing the benefits and other concerns, I accepted the offer.

Hired as executive director

So, in 1996, this nonprofit organization hired me as their executive director to administer their homebuyer education program. It was nobody but God that opened the door for me to get that position after having no experience. The job had a big title, but in the beginning, it was a one-person show. My office was located inside a bank in Bradenton. The branch manager was one of the board of directors and the bank's vice president.

Homeownership training for first-time homebuyers

The Board of Directors comprised bank vice presidents, mortgage companies, title company presidents, real estate brokers, and sometimes, Builders. Part of my job as executive director was to seek annual contributions from these organizations to support the Coalition in providing homeownership training and counseling and by contributing a certain amount entitled them to board membership.

Most counties and cities have an affordable housing program to assist low and moderate-income individuals seeking to purchase a home. And, with most of the programs, you must attend homebuyer education to qualify. A home is the most significant investment a person will make in their lifetime, and most people need help to figure out where to begin the process.

For this reason, the Coalition had a contractual agreement with the county government to provide homeownership training to first-time homebuyers seeking down payment and closing cost assistance through the county's state housing initiative program (S. H. I. P.). The organization provided education using the professionals of lenders, realtors, credit counseling services, and title companies. Many members of the Board of Directors would teach the class in their profession. This was an opportunity for them to take part in training as well as to get clients. It also motivated them to contribute to the organization.

The education provided participants with the knowledge, and skills needed to get and keep possession of their homes. Therefore, participants were required to attend eight hours of training which included; preparing for homeownership/fair housing rights, budgeting, developing a winning credit history, shopping for a home, applying for a mortgage, closing the loan, and home ownership means earned responsibility.

One board member/vice president of one bank was very instrumental in growing the organization after I came on board. She assisted me in writing a grant to the county, expanding the services to include not just homebuyer education but pre and post-purchase counseling, marketing, and outreach initiatives.

Therefore, the county approving the grant boosted our funding and allowed the organization to move into its location outside of the bank. And this same person was very influential in the organization's further growth. She had many great ideas and helped me locate a building in which the county reimbursed the coalition for the rent of the building. Also, she helped get furnishings to fill the office.

It was like setting up a business from the start. Although not experienced in creating reports, I became proficient enough to provide the necessary reports needed to provide the Board of Directors and the county government. Being determined to learn everything needed to run that office. Creating newsletters, brochures, and flyers. Thinking back, it's hard to believe I accomplished what I did. What gifts and talents we have hidden away and do not use are amazing.

However, preparing grants for funding is what I found to be very stressful, because you had time constraints, and it was not an area of expertise for me. God sent the help needed each time, for what I needed every time. Due to needing more confidence in my writing, I would have the Vice President critique any of my documents before sending out any correspondence. Then, after moving from her office, I would email those correspondences to her for her to review.

Housing counseling agency

Received a Certificate of Completion from the Neighborhood Reinvestment Training Institute for "Housing Counseling" and a certificate from the Department of Community Affairs Affordable

Housing Catalyst Program for completing "How to Manage an Affordable Housing Program."

Then, the Coalition received a certificate of approval as a housing counseling agency in 2000. Afterward, we hired an assistant, and she would assist with the classes and provide housing and credit counseling. A credit agency set us up to access credit reports, to serve the clients better when providing credit counseling. Later, the Coalition received funding to administer the county, down payment, and closing cost assistance program, which required us to attend the closings and complete portions of the closing documents.

Hundreds of individuals attended homebuyer education and received certificates during my tenure with the organization. The organization assisted many individuals with down payment and closing costs and helped them achieve the American Dream of Homeownership.

The hindrance that kept most individuals from buying a home was credit issues. Either they would need to establish credit or repair their credit. We directed those with credit issues through the steps needed to improve their credit to better position them to purchase a home. We advised those with no credit on how to establish credit.

Some individuals would find out they were not in a position due to needing more income. Many learned that they were not ready for homeownership for other reasons. Knowledge is power, and attending homeownership training educated participants to make intelligent decisions. Most found the classes to be very informative.

Backstabbing

I worked with the Coalition for seven years, and in between those years, after hiring temporary and full-time help, the backstabbing started. Staff began going behind my back and complaining to the county. The county later employed one of my employees. It was an excellent opportunity for this person because the county is a stable job with benefits. In contrast, the Coalition depended on funding from year to year. The responsibilities they hired this person to do for the county in their housing and community services department were some of the same job responsibilities she had at the Coalition. Therefore, it was an easy hire for the County.

The Coalition would have constant contact with the county on a day-to-day basis between our staff and the county staff either on the telephone or when making trips back and forth to pick up or drop off closing packets for clients receiving the down payment and closing cost assistance. Another employee was going behind my back as well. I had much trust in her and taught her many things, and she had been a big help to the organization, but she began being deceptive. She has since reached out and apologized for her actions. She called me when I was no longer employed with the Coalition and admitted she was wrong, and apologized and I forgave her.

Then, the temporary help went behind my back and complained about me during her lunch hour at a board member's office. She was not doing her job and wanted to gossip. She often returned from her lunch hour late, and I would overlook it because she was temporary help. The board member informed me of her conversation and told me the employee complained I had been completing income taxes on the job. She was also telling her other things that were not true.

My comment to the Board member was that she was correct. I would work on my taxes during my downtime. I would spend many hours at my desk and would not leave most of the time for lunch or take breaks. Classes would be from six until eight in the evenings, and I would not go home. I'm sure the board member was not expecting my honesty. She thought I would deny the accusation, therefore, she was left speechless.

This young lady did not realize that her actions exposed her deception. You can't do things like that and think people will not see your betrayal. It shows that you are not to be trusted. It ended her temporary employment, and the board member she complained to, was in favor of terminating her. You will not get very far in life if you have to go behind someone's back, telling lies, trying to get them fired, or being a tattle-tale to gain favor. It will catch up with you.

I was told this young lady had caused problems in other jobs where she'd worked. She was an intelligent woman, but a conniving one. You want to trust people, but they seem to always deceive you. People can be very deceptive, no matter how nice you try to be to them. My husband always tells me, "You do not trust anyone." That's because too many people have shown me you can't.

Tried to renege

In 2003, the Board of Directors agreed to pay me an additional ten percent of the grant amount, if awarded, to prepare and submit a HUD grant for funding. HUD awarded the grant. Then, the Board tried to renege on their agreement. It has to be assumed that when the Board agreed to pay the ten percent, they must have thought they would not award the grant. Then, when HUD awarded the funding, they came up with excuses not to pay.

They discussed getting a lawyer to look at everything. A Board member took the concern to the county and discussed it with the County staff, who said it was a board decision and expense. Unless outlined in the grant application, they cannot pay the grant writer with the grant funding. The Coalition had enough reserves to pay me without relying on the funds from the grant, so that was not the problem.

Without going through all the details, the Coalition paid me for writing the grant because of one board member who stood up and spoke out for me. After that, it was difficult for me to trust the Board after they tried to back out of an agreement. Putting that grant together required hard work, time, and commitment. Then, afterward, it was a lot of dissension, backbiting, and tearing down of the organization, as one board member expressed. There were a lot of lies and rumors being spread concerning the organization and me.

Resignation

On the first of March 2004, after much consideration, I resigned. But it was a privilege to use my skills and talents for such a worthwhile organization, educating individuals seeking to purchase a home. I then recommended an employee that would have been great for the position, but the Coalition hired a board member who had come on board.

We believe it was her intention when she joined the Board that her motivation was to seek the executive director position. She would come to visit me in the office, asking many questions. The organization went defunct after a couple of years. "Everything has its time." I was there for a season, and I loved it. God brought much creativity out of me during those years. It was a blessing.

Received my real estate license

Working with homebuyers gave me a strong interest in becoming a realtor. Therefore, I attended Ed Klopfer Schools of Real Estate, completed the sales associate pre-license course, and passed the state exam. I was not one of those fortunate enough to pass the test the first time. It took me several tries, and I would leave the test site in tears, but I was determined. I learned that only fifty percent of people would pass that state exam.

So, I received my Real Estate License in March 2004. I began as an agent in their office for this known company in Bradenton, with real estate offices throughout the County. For the month, I made top listing agents several times. Because of referrals from people who knew me from the Coalition, and someone who turned me on to a family that referred me to other family members. For a brief season, I did well.

2007 housing market crash

The 2007 housing market crash made it very hard for realtors, so I gave it up. I still have my license, but it is inactive. So, every two years, I continue to complete my fourteen hours of training. I advise anyone who wants to get a Real Estate License, to not let failing the test several times deter you. If it is something you want to accomplish, keep trying.

Independent Contractor

So, after the real estate market fell, I signed a contract with The Healthy Start Coalition that provides Community-Based Healthy Start Care Coordination and Hospital-Based Healthy Start

Care Coordination as an Independent Contractor for three years, from June 19, 2006, until June 13, 2009. Five Care Coordinators were hired. One was a mental health counselor, one a social worker, and the remaining three of us with bachelor's degrees in other fields. It was a decent beginning salary, and we all had to share the cost of monthly rent for office space.

The Healthy Start Coalition began in 1992 to implement the provision of Florida's Healthy Start Legislation within the county to help pregnant women get linked to medical providers early in their pregnancies throughout the first three years of their child's life. The program's target is pregnant women at risk for poor pregnancy outcomes and risk for poor growth and development.

Through Care Coordination, participants were eligible to receive comprehensive prenatal and child health care, childbirth education, parenting education support, nutritional, psychosocial, and smoking cessation counseling, breastfeeding education and support, home visiting, and other services.

During my three-year contract, the hospital-based healthy start care coordination was most of my workload in the hospital after the infant was

born and before they discharged the mother. I
would get referrals from the hospital after a
mother's release if they felt a risk for the child or
mother. I provided patient information and educated
the mother on the awareness of (SID) Sudden Infant
Death before taking her child home. Along with
other parenting information.

I would make sure the mother had access to a
crib if we did not provide her with one and other
needed items. I would refer the participant to other
organizations for needs. Most cases I would
encounter would be closed out when I left the
hospital visit because no further services were
needed. Open cases would be closed because of
being unable to locate participants. Some at-risk
participants may have felt you would intrude in
their life and may not have wanted that because so
many would not respond to your attempts to reach
them. Healthy Start would also provide families
with Christmas gifts, pampers, clothing, and more.
Therefore, it is a worthwhile organization.

I was doing my job to the best of my ability.
The job entailed much more than described here.
But for me, getting the participants beyond the
hospital visit was challenging. I just did not feel
satisfied that I had truly helped someone when I

would go home daily. Even though the salary was decent, I declined to renew my contract as an independent contractor for another three years.

Part-time teller

Bored of being at home and not working, I continued to check out job openings. It appears to be a habit. Therefore, around September 2011, there was an opening for a part-time teller with a bank across from our home. Since it was close to our house, I decided I would apply. It was a new branch open only for a short time.

When I was called and offered the job, I accepted it. In this role, you were required to attend two weeks of training at one of their locations in Tampa. After passing the teller training, although I had worked in several banks, the training activities I found a little complicated.

However, my employment began with the bank on November 13, 2011. When I started, the teller line included the assistant branch manager/teller, two other tellers, and myself. With it being a new branch, business was a little slow. Everything was going well, and I was doing the job as required. So, there was a desk and a chair behind the teller line, and this one teller would sit there all the time. If he was not there, then I would sit because I had been in a car accident and would experience sciatic back pain.

Requires standing

I came to work one day, and someone had removed the chair. As a result, I inquired about it and was told by the acting assistant branch manager that the regional manager does not want chairs behind the teller line because we are required to stand. I asked him if he expected me to stand during training on the computer, and he commented, "No, you can use the station when sitting down." Later, I spoke with the branch manager about the situation, and she stated, "The job requires standing."

As a result, I informed her that after standing for long periods of time, I would get pain in my hip and lower back. She stated I needed to consider whether the job as a teller would be for me and to think about it before going to Tampa the following day for additional training. In response, she was told; I would need to think about it because I could not continue to stand all the time. I told her I wish they had informed me that the job required standing before I accepted it.

Disability and reasonable accommodation

Later, I asked her if I could give a two-week notice because I had always given a two-week notice before leaving a job. So, she told me I could. However, the teller, who normally would sit in the chair and who was getting ready to leave the bank and go to another job, overheard what was happening. He pulled up the policy on disability and reasonable accommodation and had me to read it. Then, after I read it, I tried to call the number they had written for you to call, which was the Employee Relations Executive number.

However, there was no answer when I made the call. So, In the meantime, the branch manager came to me and asked me what was I doing and then said she would pay me. I assumed she meant she would pay me for two weeks after I gave my notice if I were to leave. Therefore, after reading the policy, I told her I was trying to contact the Employee Relations Executive number. With an attitude, she stood up and informed me to make the call.

I tried the number again and got through to a gentleman who instructed me to contact my doctor's office and get medical certification showing my condition. He informed me to contact this person at the bank and provided me with her telephone number. He also told me this lady would inform me where to send the documentation. The gentleman called the branch manager and spoke with her.

Later, the branch manager called me into her office, and the acting assistant branch manager was also present. She asked me if I was resigning, and I told her, "No, not after reading the policy." She then asked, "Are you rescinding?" I said "yes," based on the information that was provided to me.

She said, "Let me reiterate, you will be required to stand until you get the medical documents." She also said, "When you go to Tampa, I will pay your mileage, not your lunch." Later, I provided the Employee Relations Department with the requested documents, and the bank ordered a chair for me to sit in.

Didn't go over very well

Because of the Disability and Reasonable Accommodation Policy, the situation did not go over well with the regional manager after being contacted by his superior regarding how the branch manager addressed the issue. If the bank violated the Disability and Reasonable Accommodation Policy rules and guidelines, I could have held the bank liable. Indeed, the branch manager held the situation unprofessional. She took it personally and tried to show her power in her position.

She, along with other branch managers, was expecting a big bonus. According to her, it cost her twenty thousand dollars. That's how much she was expecting to get for her bonus. Due to how she reacted to the situation, she did not get it. I was so thankful God used that young man to make me aware of that policy, otherwise, the branch manager would have tried to force me to resign, and she did not have that right. Her attitude towards me was nasty. As a result, she ended her employment a few months later.

The odd thing about it was that the teller who was leaving would sit in that chair all the time. It wasn't until I started sitting in the chair that it became an issue. But I think this teller complained to the assistant branch manager about it. The assistant branch manager was close to the branch manager, and after everything went down with her, he wanted me out of there. He had been trying to find a reason to write me up for no cause, therefore he did not give me a fair review, despite my always balancing and being a great customer service employee.

When the young man left, his position got replaced by this attractive young girl. Because she was an appealing young woman, favoritism started between the male workers and this young girl. So, she would be on her telephone, and it was no problem, but I would get harassed by the assistant branch manager during the slow times for reading my bible.

A higher bonus

He continued trying to find things to harass me about. We had this promotion going on based on customer reviews of their interaction with an employee; our branch could get a bronze, silver, or gold bonus. So, the assistant branch manager/head teller would make slick comments, insinuating that the branch wasn't getting a bronze because of me. He would run around the office, being fake and overly friendly to customers. For months, we could never reach our goal. They moved him to another office. Once he left, the office got a gold status, and we received a higher bonus. But, he had been blaming me for why we never received the gold status.

I sent a letter to the regional manager expressing my disappointment with how the temporary assistant branch manager favored the attractive young girl and would allow her to work all openings for a week. I would have to do the closings. Then, he increased her hours when we were slow. She started the job after I started, but was getting her way with everything. The temporary assistant branch manager would always be at her teller window fraternizing. It began causing low employee morale because I couldn't compete with a pretty young girl despite being great at customer service and balancing. It just wasn't fair, however, we experience this all the time.

Last day of employment

October 29, 2012, was my last day of employment. Once I purchased our little Milo from a customer, I completed my work there. Milo continues to make our day and bring us so much happiness. My season there was over after one year. Since then, I have not worked. God is good. Everything has its time. I am reminded of the scripture, *To me belongeth vengeance, and recompense; Their foot shall slip in due time; For the day of their calamity is at hand, And the things that shall come upon them make haste* (Deut. 32:35 KJV).

Chapter Thirteen

Gambling

Glitzy and glamorous inside

In my life, I was always economically conscious of money and was more of a thrifty spender. It was this one person who would tease me and tell people that I probably still had the first dollar I'd earned. She knew how serious I was about saving money. My son told me once, "Mom, you always buy things on sale; when I get older, I'm going to buy whatever I want." It was always a habit for me to save money, but not to the point that I would not give to others in need.

However, in 2007, my husband and I visited the Tampa Hard Rock and Casino. I can't remember the occasion if there was one. Immediately, I fell in love with being there once we entered the building. We see all these people walking around, some sitting at slot machines, card games, and roulette tables. The slot machines were lit up, and some were sounding off. There were gorgeous light fixtures all around. The place was glitzy and glamorous inside. It was an unfamiliar experience and thrilling. We walked around enjoying the scenery.

A disturbing habit

Then, I tried my luck putting money into one of the slot machines, not realizing that this would be the start of years of a disturbing habit. We started going on weekends. Therefore, it became our weekend entertainment. We would win, and we would lose, and during our time there, we met a lot of different people. They were from all professions and all walks of life. They would be visiting from all over Florida, as well as from other states and countries. People would be from everywhere.

In 2009, when they held the Super Bowl in Tampa, Fl., the Hard Rock took in lots of money, and they were paying out big money for a few years. We were winning a lot, and we were winning big; it was time to dance. Nevertheless, the thing with gambling; with myself and most people I have witnessed, is that when you win, there is something in your mind that triggers you to continue to sit at the machine until you have played back all of what you have won. Then, if you do not play your winnings back at that time, you will have the urge to come back and get right back on the machine or another one until you have given it all back, then some, because you are thinking you are going to win again.

Therefore, we continued to go there, thinking we would get back some of what we lost, only to lose more and more. You realize you can never get ahead, but you continue to fool yourself, thinking you will hit it big one day. Also, the casino is good at what they do with those machines. When you are at the last few hits before running out of money, the machine will start showing the possibility of big hits to entice you to continue to play. Although you know you are just giving them your money. You would get so caught up that you could spend hours there and lose track of time gambling. I had a relative tell me that the buildings in casinos are purposely designed with no windows to look out and no clocks to see the time, so you can only focus on gambling and giving them your money.

Offering promotions

Casinos make it seem appealing by offering promotions like hotel stays and giveaways like cars, trucks, SUVs, and motorcycles to reel you in. We have been seeing an advertisement on television with this woman we met at the Hard Rock. We met her and her husband. She is excited on the commercial because she won a BMW. I would be also, but she has paid the casino for that BMW many times over.

The Casino provides member players with comps. Comps are complimentary items and services from casinos to encourage players to gamble. The amount and quality of comps a player is given depend on what game(s) they play, how much they bet, and how long they play. Complimentary can be free play or eating at restaurants, purchasing items at their stores, gifts, gift cards, or other services they provide. Therefore, when you get hungry, there are different places to choose from to dine. Some people only come to the casino to eat at their restaurants, which range from inexpensive to expensive. So, we received many comps and would enjoy spending our downtime eating at the Fresh Harvest Restaurant.

The Fresh Harvest Buffet restaurant has seven live kitchens and various food options. The actor Jaleel White, who plays Erkel, was seen there dining with friends. We also saw Roman Reigns, the professional wrestler and his family dining, and several professional football players. I also ran into the football player Dion Sander's mother and took a picture with her. So, you never know whom you will run into while being there. Again, it was exciting.

Continued year after year

This habit continued year after year. As a result, I went as far as to ban myself from the casino for one year, only to wear dark shades under disguise or to go to their Hollywood, Fl. or Kissimmee, Fl., location to gamble. Then, I banned myself for five years only to do the same thing. As usual, you would witness people win thousands of dollars, only to see them play it all back, or, like me, you would continue to come back to the casino and play until you have given it all back.

This one lady won, as I recall, one point one million on the Wheel of Fortune machine. When we returned there a few days later; she had about five Wheel of Fortune machines reserved and was playing each one of them. No one else was allowed to play them because she had the casino to rope them off. She thought she would win that one point one million again. Therefore, she continued to come back until she played back all her winnings. Then, after a few months, we no longer would see her anymore.

Prayer for both of us

As a result, you would hear stories of individuals' struggles. I was sitting next to this young lady playing on the slot machine, and she shared with me how she lost everything because of gambling. She told me she had lost her husband and her home. She said she would be there sometimes all night, and her husband started spending time with another woman. I then asked her if she would mind me praying for her, and she responded, "No, I do not." I held her hand and prayed for the both of us as we sat at the slot machine.

Then, another young lady, she and I became acquainted. We would sometimes talk together on the telephone about our desire to break the addiction. Every time I would see her at the casino, she would have the same complaint; she had spent her entire check or bill money and could not go home, because her husband would be mad at her. It would not stop her. I just continued to hear her talk about her husband's threats to divorce her whenever I ran into her. When you would see her most of the time, she asked to loan her money and would never pay it back. So, she finally banned herself from the casino for a year, which I have done twice. It does not do any good. You can still go there, but they will not allow you to get the money if you win a jackpot. Also, they can escort you out of the casino. Since then speaking with her, she has started going back. She is an intelligent woman with a career who earns decent money but struggles with addiction.

Another time, this lady in 2011, her husband took her to the casino for their anniversary, and she became hooked. Having access to her in-law's money, she stole 500,000 from their life savings. After winning nearly 13 million from the Seminole Hard Rock Casino in Tampa, she pumped every penny of that back in, plus at least $700.000 more, according to the article. Charged with 16 counts, including exploitation of the elderly, forgery of checks, and organized scheme to defraud. After being convicted, she did prison time.

Another friend I met at the Casino struggled with her marriage because she spent much time at the casino. Due to other reasons, as well as wanting her freedom to gamble, she wanted a divorce. Eventually, they divorced, and the proceeds were split after selling their home together. So, she moved back into a house she also owned. Once she received her split from their home sale, she started returning to the casino.

The worst thing you can do

While the divorce was going through, she stopped going to the casino because she did not want her gambling to reflect on the outcome of the divorce. She was winning and losing. I would tell her, "You know, the worst thing you can do is hit those jackpots." She had hit plenty of them, big and small. Therefore, I would advise her not to give it back. She would say, "I want." When I would talk with her again, she'd say, "Yea, girl, I gave it all back." Sometimes she'd say, "I bought a little back." We would have these conversations over and over. She has gone back, and she has lost more and more. I was guilty of that same pattern.

She told me she had lost so much one day; she went back the next day thinking she would get some of her money back and found herself deeper indebted. It may take her a while, but she will get it. No matter how often we are warned, it's not that easy for some of us.

It appears to be much deeper than greed. I would sit and put hundreds into the machine. Being a thrifty spender would be far from my mind at the casino. For some reason, it would not faze me how much I was spending until I'd left. Then, I would think about what I could have done with the money I've spent. The experience is like something takes over you. I would advise no one to gamble because it could become addictive. Some people have a strong will and can win and leave. There were times I could hold on to my winnings, and times when I could not. After hitting the jackpot, I would be on a binge to come back and play some more. Someone referred to it as being like a drug. We were not the type to go there every day, but when I was on that binge, we would go a couple of times a week.

Gambling had become a struggle

Most people who visit casinos are gamblers and need help. We were spending all of our savings. Gambling had become a struggle. Some people we have met at the casino have passed away. For some, the stress of gambling and losing their money may have caused illnesses that may have taken them out. Although you do not hear about it, gambling is a serious problem. If you are interested, you can read about gambling addictions. This acquaintance told me about a young woman gambling at the card table who was devastated over the amount she had lost and had a heart attack at the table. They took her to the hospital, where she demised.

Most gamblers who have won large amounts will tell you they do not know where that money has gone. We stopped going as much as we used to. I kept telling my husband that there was a reason we were not winning anymore. In the last several years, it seemed the casino was controlling the machines, making it difficult for you to win. The one blessing with us was that gambling never prevented us from handling our responsibilities at home. Thanks to God for having his hedge of protection all around us during this time. He protected us, keeping us from total financial ruin.

The last time we were there and returned home, pulling into the driveway, plain and clear it came to me to write a book. Since that revelation, we never went back to the casino and I got involved in writing this book. I wanted to obey the notion that was laid on my heart. I had been praying for God to heal me from the addiction. Everything has its time. We had a long gambling season before God removed it. He already knew when He was going to heal me. It was in His timing. I knew gambling was wrong, but there is a purpose for everything. Whatever the adversary meant for my harm, God will turn it around for my good, and He will get all the glory. I have advised my friends who are struggling to keep praying, God will deliver them in His time.

For the thing I greatly feared has come upon me, and what I dreaded has happened to me (Job 3:25 NKJV). My obsession with saving money and my fear of being without it, God has allowed me to depart from it, but he continues to take care of us. *And my God shall supply all your need according to His riches in glory by Christ Jesus* (Phil. 4:19 KJV). Therefore, we do not need anything other than God, because He will supply our every need. He already has things in motion for us to get back everything we have lost and more. God is an awesome God and deserves our highest praise. *To every thing there is a season, and a time to every purpose under the heaven: a time to get and a time to lose*; (Eccles. 3:1, 6a KJV).

Gambling can be devastating because you can lose everything. There is help for anyone who feels they may need it. The Florida Council on Compulsive Gambling; free resources are available by calling the 24/7, Confidential, and Multilingual Problem Gambling Helpline at 888-ADMIT-IT (236-4848).

Chapter Fourteen

The Truth

For nothing is secret

So, after my father's death, my sister would continue to tell me how much I looked like my mother. She seemed to have become obsessed with telling me this. I've heard it all my life, and so has my sister about looking like her dad. However, she continued telling me this as though there was a message.

According to the verse (Luke 8:17 KJV), *for nothing is secret, that shall not be made manifest; neither anything hid, that shall not be known and come abroad.* Everything has its time.

My sister and her son had taken the Ancestry DNA test. So, curiosity got the best of me. Therefore, I ordered the kit and was tested. My

DNA results came back around August 2018, and at that time, it was determined that my sister and I were half-sisters… we did not share the same father. Therefore, I've learned the truth about something I've questioned all my life. My father/dad was not my biological father. This was discovered two years after my father passed away. It was devastating to find out he was not my natural father. Then, there were more questions… did his family know this all along?

It doesn't always mean someone is not your parent because you look more like one than the other. But, some physical features from the mother and father will show up as their child grows up. However, there was no resemblance at all between my dad and me. Now, my sister no longer tells me how much I look like my mom. She didn't know why she continued to repeat it, but she was not expecting that outcome. But the truth has a way of manifesting itself.

Although the truth has just been unveiled to me, it's likely that my dad already knew that. I just did not know. I know he had been in my life from the time I had been born. I was told he was my father, and I honestly believed it. But through the years, I had my reservations because of how he

treated me. He never wanted to do anything for me.
He would treat my sister differently. In a discussion
I had with someone after finding out the truth, they
told me my dad knew the truth deep down, even if
he did not divulge it to me. For whatever reason,
God allowed that truth to remain until after his
death. That I find to be amazing because it further
deepens my realization of *"Everything Has Its
Time."* I still loved my father/dad, and it did not
change my feelings for him. He was still my dad,
the only dad I knew.

On A Mission

Still, that deception hurts. I've now been on a
mission to discover my biological father. Some
people do not care to know, but I would like to learn
who my natural father is/was. However, this young
man appears on my DNA matches as a close
relative. He is 59%, possibly a great-grand-nephew
on my father's side. And after contacting the young
man, I learned he was related to a family on his
mother's side that I am familiar with in the town I
grew up.

Although this young man lives in Smyrna,
Georgia, and grew up in Colorado Springs, Co. I
contacted one of their local family members, and
she shared with me that this young man was the

grandson of one of their relatives. Trying to determine if their family was related to me, I'd asked a few family members if they would take the DNA test if I made the purchase, and two agreed. A couple of them that were asked, did not care to take the test. However, the two that took the DNA test did not show up under my DNA matches. Therefore, the family was eliminated as being relatives.

Then, further DNA research showed the young man was related to me by two different families. The two families would have to be my father's mother's side of the family and the other his father's side of the family. So far he is the only close match where we are related to both families, which is definitely vital information that could lead to who my father is. Contrary to the information on Ancestry that connects him to these two families, he has no clue how he's related to them.

He'd told me he could not provide me with much information because his mother, who is my age, passed away in July 2012. Her mother, who raised him and once lived in the town where I'd grown up, passed away in 2014. And he doesn't know very much about his family on his father's side. Even though his mother and father were married and divorced, he said he and his father do not communicate. They'd divorced when he was younger. He told me his father's name and that he had three half-sisters from his father and provided me with their names.

"I don't know those people"

That being said, with the information, I researched his father's telephone number. After calling the number, his father's mother answered the telephone. When speaking with the mother, she was made aware that I'd spoken with her grandson and that he was a close relative to me based on Ancestry DNA. She was surprised I'd had a conversation with him because, according to her, they had not been in contact with each other for many years.

However, she wanted to know how I'd gotten her telephone number, which was expected. My response was… from the directory of white pages. Then, I informed her of the two last names I'd been seeking information about. Her comment was, "I don't know those people." On the other hand, her concern was knowing about me, my mother, and where we were from. She was not interested in giving out any information. So, in the meantime, it is a dead end for now.

Contacting and speaking with a male relative whose DNA shows he is a second cousin or 1st cousin 2x removed encouraged me to purchase their 2018 Family History book that could be bought from Amazon. At first, a little hesitant about buying the book, but glad I did. I've since found several relatives' names in the book that are DNA matches to me on Ancestry. The book is well-written with beautiful photos and has the names of their descendants. But, on December 16, 2020, this relative passed away. He was a very distinguished man looking at his photos in the book. He'd been married five times and had five sons and before he passed away, he had a fiancé. After reading their family history book, I learned their family was from Columbia County, Georgia.

It's in the DNA

According to the book, his grandfather was a pastor known for his preaching and leading souls to Christ. In business and personal matters, he was a negotiator for his people with the white community. It states, as quoted in the Augusta Chronicle on September 25, 1936, "Rev. was one of the outstanding ministers in the county and state of Georgia. He was always ready and eager to help anyone experiencing distress or grief, and the examples he set as a law-abiding citizen and accumulating property is worth emulating." It appears he'd be my great-grandfather. He had twelve children. One of his sons is the father of the male relative I spoke with whose DNA shows he is a 2nd cousin or 1st cousin 2x removed. The history book has written that family members have excelled in many professions. That information is good to know. Even though I did not get to know those who have passed away or to know those that are alive personally, I see their photos in the book. They are my blood relatives, it's in the DNA and nothing can change that.

On the other family side, a young lady is a close DNA match, and she is 68% a 1st cousin 2x removed. After asking her if she'd ask her dad to take the Ancestry DNA if I purchased it, she did, and he agreed. His DNA showed he is 84% a first cousin 1x removed. So, with that, he is the closest DNA match to me that has taken the test on my father's side.

According to a family tree, his father's brother's (my grand-uncle) daughter, who would be my first cousin 1x removed, died on April 17, 2020, at 86 years old. Her obituary indicates she earned a Ph.D. from New York University and was

recognized as an educator and author. Many awards
she has earned. A member of Alpha Kappa Alpha
Sorority, Inc. Her husband was an attorney, and
they had three sons who would be my 2nd cousins
or 1st cousins 2x removed. After googling one of
her sons, according to Encyclopedia.com, he is a
New York University PH.D. And states CAREER:
Teacher, poet, anthologist, consultant, and lecturer.

Migrated north

The family was out of Blackville, Barnwell,
South Carolina, and their grandfather had 11
children. They all migrated north to New Jersey,
Philadelphia, and New York. The families are large.
So, this is why it is so difficult to trace back who
my father is unless someone closer who's related to
him somehow ends up taking the DNA test.
Therefore, it is a mystery now, but I'm not willing
to give up. I used to tell people I have few cousins,
but now I've discovered many DNA matches.

However, this situation does not reflect who
my mother was, I'm sure she did what she had to
do, like many women. She was an admirable
woman and I would not trade her for the world. She
made mistakes with her choices of men that caused
her a lot of heartache and pain, but many women
can identify with that. No one can judge her.

But, it does hurt thinking one person is your father and finding out he isn't after all these years. I loved my dad and treated him like a daughter, even if he was not my father. I'm determined though, to know who my biological father was/is, and it is my goal not to give up on my search to find him. If I do not, at least I have the truth. Everything has its time.

Chapter Fifteen

The Person I Am

Put my trust in God and not man

My mother inspired us and helped shape me into the person I am today. She taught me to put my trust in God and not in man. She taught me how to be a woman, how I'm to treat my husband, how to raise my children, how to work for what I want, and about having integrity, among many other things.

My mother's extravagance and her desire to buy expensive things made me somewhat the opposite. In fact, she would shop for my sister and me in expensive stores for shoes and clothing however, most of the time, I would not wear them. She had to pay more for my shoes because of my

215

narrow feet. My sister and I were spoiled, perhaps because my mother had all boys first. Do not get me wrong, I love nice things, but they do not have to be expensive.

Therefore, quality over expensive is what I'd look for, and getting what I buy at a reasonable price. An "on-sale shopper," I've considered myself. More so, a clearance shopper, because sometimes, on-sale is not on-sale enough for me. There is nothing wrong with having nice things, that's what I grew up with, but you have to have restraints. Some people like to keep up with the Joneses and try to impress people or try to build an image to think highly of themselves. Impressing people, I do not feel a need.

We must be cautious because we live in a competitive society where everyone tries to outdo one another at any expense. One of those people, I try not to be. Keeping up with someone else is not a part of who I am. Just being me and staying in my lane is who I am. The world is so full of vain people needing attention, so-called... In the name of Jesus. *2For men will be lovers of themselves, lovers of money, boasters, proud, blasphemers, disobedient to parents, unthankful, unholy, 3unloving, unforgiving, slanderers, without self-control, brutal,*

despisers of good, 4traitors, headstrong, haughty,
lovers of pleasure rather than lovers of
God, 5having a form of godliness but denying its
power. And from such people turn away! (2 Tim. 3:
2-5 NKJV). Amen.

Doubled-over position

Many acquaintances I've had, but few friends
and fewer close friends. I haven't had a close friend
consistently throughout my life. I've rekindled a
friendship with a friend I met in junior college, and
we have been close. I'd not seen this friend in many
years because she had moved away.

When she and I had a chance to see one
another, it wasn't what I expected. Because of
several car accidents, she had been going through a
lot with her health, and she and her husband had
separated. Because of pain, she was in a doubled-
over position and could not stand straight up. For
several years, she said she was in a wheelchair and
had to walk with a walker. It was painful watching
her. She looked nothing like the friend I'd met years
ago in junior college.

After experiencing so much pain, and being
told her condition was getting worse, she decided to
have back surgery. The surgery, she was told, could

be very risky and leave her paralyzed. She had to undergo two procedures, one on May 9, 2022, and another on May 11, 2022. There were complications afterward, which God brought her through. For thirteen years or more, she said, she'd suffered from being doubled over and struggling with the pain,

What made her decide to have the surgery was that she wanted to attend her daughter's wedding and be able to stand up straight. Also, she wanted to be able to dance. Therefore, she prayed to God about it. God answered her prayer on November 11, 2022. She'd sent the video of her and her estranged husband, (which was another blessing) dancing at their daughter's wedding. My friend looked beautiful.

She had faith that God would bring her through that surgery, and He did. God allowed me to reconnect with her and be in her life during this time for a reason. For the last three or four years, I'd been around while she was going through some of her trials and saw her having her faith tested. I was a witness to what God did for her. There is a purpose for everything. Prayer changes things. My friend has been praying and what she has been praying for, God is working it all out in His time because "Everything has its time."

Please forgive me

Saying this with humility, I've always been a person that is direct, straightforward, and to the point. I have a strong personality. I'm not someone who sugarcoats what I need to say. Because of that, people will perceive you the wrong way. We are all unique individuals. God made us all different. So, people will judge you even before they get to know you.

My family has told me I'm pessimistic, critical, mean-spirited, judgmental, and argumentative. Recently, evil has been added, but my husband and daughter, who knows me will tell you differently. I've never been an evil person… that I know. Perhaps a little mean at times and most women have their mean streaks. I'm a child of God. God loves me just as I am; just as he loves everyone else. No one is perfect and nowhere near it.

Therefore, we do not have to accept the labels people try to put on us. God does not judge us like people, even though we do have to be careful we are not behaving as the bible tells us not to. We are human and sin daily in words, thoughts, and deeds. When we do, we are to ask God for forgiveness, and when we ask for forgiveness, we have to believe He has forgiven us and not let what people say condemn us because they will try to.

People telling me what to do, I'd always had a problem with that. Pray for me, I do not know why. I'm someone that considers myself a leader and not a follower. I can be controlling, it's a part of my makeup... please forgive me. I'm also, a person who always thinks the worst, and I do that to prepare myself because of my experiences in life. I'm a sensitive person who gets upset easily, which stems from being picked on and called names when I was younger. I'm someone who speaks my mind when upset, which comes from having to defend myself growing up. As well as I am opinionated; please forgive me. I'd been told I can give criticism... but can't take it, I accept that. I'd been told it was my tone. God is still working on me.

I've always been persistent and determined. Once I start something, I won't stop until it's finished. I've always been impatient, and it has cost me. It is one reason I have had so many jobs. You lose in different ways when you are impatient. Even though I've worked all my life, I missed out on long-term benefits like pensions. Therefore, I continue to pray for patience. But, it could have all been a part of God's Plan for my life.

His word says, *And we know all things work together for good to those who love God, to those who are the called according to His purpose* (Romans 8:28 NKJV). We do not know what someone has gone through that makes them react as they do. When we hear the saying, "If you can walk a mile in my shoes," maybe, you will better understand. Some things weigh heavy on your heart, like raising one of my son's daughters whose mother I begged not to become pregnant at 16. Her sister, my other grandchild, I did not raise. My son and their mother being on drugs, allowed someone else to care for her. I did not disagree with it when I found out, because I did not want to bring up another child. We'd visit her, and we stayed connected. She was well provided for by the family who raised her. She is grown now and has her own child.

We continue to help our granddaughter who lived with us raise her son, whom she had at an early age and was born with a heart condition called Shone Complex. We'd been told he would have six heart surgeries; so far, he has only had two, and we thank God. He had open heart surgery in 2007 and again in 2015. Contacting the same praying woman to pray for my great-grandchild, whom I'd reached out for prayer for my mother when she needed it. I believe her prayers and others have gotten him this far. He is still not out of the woods with his condition, however, he is doing okay. It frightens him now that he is older that it could be a possibility he has to have open heart surgery again. This was tough on my granddaughter, because she was young, and we were taking him back and forth to the doctors in another county. However, prayer does change things, and God helped me to remain resilient through it all.

Offenses

About six years ago, our church had a women's night event. Being the speaker, I spoke on offenses from the scripture (Luke 17:1 KJV), *"Then said he unto the disciples, it is impossible but that offenses will come: but woe to him, through whom they come!"* That message was for me because I've struggled with being offended and living on the defense. As well as offend others, but not intentionally. I'd pray for God to help me overcome it because I can't do it alone. Sometimes we will offend someone and not even realize it, and there are times someone will offend us and they will not know it. That's why God warns us; that offense will come.

God says, woe to him, through whom Offenses come, meaning through our transgressions, we are not to be stumbling blocks in the way of others. We are not to hinder anyone through our behavior, causing God's believers to slip and fall. God knows we are not perfect; therefore, through His Grace and Mercy, we are forgiven when we repent and ask for His forgiveness and we are to forgive others, no matter how many times they mess up.

*Then Peter came to him, and said, "Lord, how often shall my brother sin against me, and I forgive him? Up to seven times?" Jesus said to him, "I do not say to you, up to seven times but, up to seventy times seven" (*Matthew 18:21-22 NKJV*).*

I love people, and I love helping people. People who get to know me will find out that I'm a kind person. They will know I'm a giver and not a receiver, and for that, I'm grateful. My husband says I do too much for people. It is my nature, but I won't let anyone take advantage of me.

Being raised in the church to fear God and to put my trust in him is what I'm committed to doing. I'd always known I had a calling in my life, but the adversary has tried to distract me in many ways. I'm refusing to be defeated by him. When I'd think about my life, God has kept me and brought me through many things. For His strength and fortitude, I thank Him. Those prayers by my mother and grandmother have protected me. My siblings, I'm sure, can attest God has brought them out or kept them out of some things as well.

All six of my mother's children are still alive and well. I'd pray for my family for God to continue to station His angels of protection all around them, keeping them safe from seen and unseen dangers, and for God to bring them closer to Him. I pray to God, for Him to remove any negative behaviors mentioned if I'm thought of as having them. If I'd hindered anyone with offenses, please forgive me. It is not my intention to hurt anyone through my thoughts, words, or deeds. I haven't done everything right in my life, but one thing I'm sure of... is having the favor of God in my life. *1 To every thing there is a season, and a time to every purpose under the heaven:* (Eccles. 3:1 KJV).

Conclusion

All in all, my having a child at a young age did not stop me from moving forward and living a fulfilled life. It was a part of God's plan. Then considering the emotional stress my mother was put through and the physical stress she endured from working so hard through the years... she is no longer suffering. With her last husband, my stepfather, in the end, he reaped what he sowed. For both, it was a difficult lesson to learn that the grass is not always greener on the other side.

God healed my second oldest brother 65 years ago... because of his faith, he is still alive today. My grandmother's son returned home alive from the military after she displayed tremendous faith and would not accept the military telling her he was dead. God allowed her to see him again for a while... then removed him from his sufferings of PTSD and alcohol abuse with his early death. God knew her sister, my grandaunt no longer wanted to live after she would not be able to continue to raise her great-grandnephew, and He called her home. God knows what is best for us, even when he brings us home to be with him. He will deliver us from all of our troubles.

After finally coming to the realization that my insecurities and self-consciousness, as well as always being on the defensive, were a result of being picked on and called names by my brothers, except the oldest and others has helped me to overcome it. Then, the trials with our marriage could've led to a divorce, however, God heard our prayers and changed things. With this in mind, God knew all about my son's sufferings, and he no longer has to struggle with life anymore after his tragic death. Our daughter being a young woman continues to go through her trials and tribulations, and for this purpose, we encourage her and remind her that God will never leave or forsake her.

God continued to show me who He was when He brought me through the challenges I experienced in my many jobs. The truth revealed, put me on the path to finding out who my biological father is/was. Then, being healed by God of gambling after He placed it on my heart to write a book. All is well, these life experiences have again, shaped me and made me the individual I am, and prepared me to be obedient to God and give these testimonies. His word says; *many are the afflictions of the righteous: but the LORD delivers him out of them all* (Psalm 34:19 NKJV). I am grateful for everything God has allowed me to go through, everything He has done in my life, and everything He has shown me in life. I have to keep in mind that: *1 To every thing there is a season, and a time to every purpose under the heaven: 2a time to be born, and a time to die; a time to plant, and a time to pluck up that which is planted; 3a time to kill, and a time to heal; a time to break down, and a time to build up; 4a time to weep, and a time to laugh; a time to mourn, and a time to dance; 5a time to cast away stones, and a time to gather stones together; a time to embrace, and a time to refrain from embracing; 6a time to get, and a time to lose; a time to keep, and a time to cast away; 7a time to rend, and a time to sew; a time to keep silence, and a time to speak; 8a time to love, and a time to hate; a time of war, and a time of peace* (Eccles 3:1-8 KJV). God knows the reasons, and we can trust He is working out His perfect plan for our good and His purpose. He sees the whole picture.

I Thank God for everything because there is a purpose for everything, and "Everything Has Its Time."

Thanks, to all my readers. God bless us all, Amen.

References

Ancestry.com http://www.ancestry.com

Allison, Christopher. Have A Gambling Problem? Florida Council on Compulsive Gambling. (2008-2019) Retrieved October 4, 2022, from https://gamblinghelp.org

Barbizon Modeling. "Barbizon International Inc." "n.d." Retrieved May 9, 2022, from https://www.barbizonmodeling.com/

Dr. Bawanna Bostic "n.d." [LinkedIn] Retrieved on December 20, 2022 from (5) Dr. Bawanna Bostic | LinkedIn

Brockman, J (2001). Jamara Clark, The other dream. *The Herald* 12 May, pg. 3

Canning, A & Hopper, J (April 8, 2011). Florida Woman Gambles $14 Million, Accused of Stealing from In-Laws. [TV Broadcasting] ABC News

Colonneso, Angelino A. "Public Records Hub"
Manatee County Clerk Of the Circuit Court and
Comptroller. Retrieved on various dates from
https://records.manateeclerk.com

Department of the Air Force. (April 22, 1988).
[Letter from Jerome C. Thies to Dorothy
Whitaker, 1988]

Dodson, Byron (2021). Tom Joyner and Adora Obi
Nwweze receive honorary doctorates from
FAMU. *Tallahassee Democrat* 30 July.

Encyclopedia. *Strickland, Michael R.* 1965- "n.d."
retrieved from
*https://www.encyclopedia.com/arts/educational-
magazines/strickland-michael-r-1965*

Forst, Erin. "Florida Delinquent Property Taxes."
Forst Tax. (2022, July 26). Retrieved June 14,
2022, from https://forst.tax/florida-delinquent-
property-taxes/

Hill, Duncan. "Comps (Casino)" "n.d." In
Wikipedia.
https://en.m.wikipedia.org/wiki/Comps/ (casino)

Kruis, J.G. (1998). *Quick Scripture Reference for
Counseling.* Baker Books

National Healthy Start Association. "Healthy Start Initiative" "n.d." Retrieved, September 27, 2022, from https://www.nationalhealthystart.org/healthy-start-initiative/

Office of Head Start. "Head Start Services" The Administration for Children and Families (2022, June 23). Retrieved, October 4, 2022, from https://www.acf.hhs.gov/ohs/about/head-start

Osteen, J. (Author) (Various Dates) Various Messages "[Radio Broadcasting]." Joel Osteen Radio

Perry, T. (Director). (2006). *Madea's Family Reunion* [Film].

Tyler Perry Studios, Reuben Cannon Productions (Perry, T. 2006)

Schardl, K. (2001). 'Groovin' on' *Tallahassee Democrat* 22 April, pg. 3, 4

Scriptures YouVersion Bible App - YouVersion

The Star-Ledger (*Dorothy S. Strickland, Ph.D.*) "n.d." Retrieved from https://obits.nj.com/us/obituaries/starledger/name/dorothy-strickland-obituary?id=8734592

References

The Tutt Family History Family, A Link to Our Past A Bridge to our Future, First Edition (2018) Book

Willie Clark (American Football). (2022, March 3). In Wikipedia. https://en.m.wikipedia.org/wiki/Willie_Clark.(American_football).

CPSIA information can be obtained
at www.ICGtesting.com
Printed in the USA
LVHW052141180723
752849LV00034B/682